APPROACHES TO THE STUDY OF INTERNATIONAL RELATIONS

POLEMOLOGICAL STUDIES
edited by Prof. Dr. B. V. A. Röling

Publications of the Polemological Institute at the University of Groningen

Polemologische Studiën, onder redactie van Prof. Mr. B. V. A. Röling
Publicaties van het Polemologisch Instituut aan de Rijksuniversiteit te Groningen

---

1. De oorlog in het licht der wetenschappen (Eerste serie)

2. Approaches to the study of international relations, 2nd. edition by Dr. Ch. Boasson

3. De oorlog in het licht der wetenschappen (Tweede serie)

4. Aspecten van de koude oorlog

5. Opstand en revolutie

6. Economische gevolgen van ontwapening door Dr. W. F. Duisenberg

7. World Peace through World Economy. Selected studies in the problems of creating a world economic order. Introduced by professor Jan Tinbergen

8. Inleiding tot de wetenschap van oorlog en vrede

9. Nieuw-Guinea en de Volkskrant door Dr. C. V. Lafeber

10. Revolutie in Latijns-Amerika

11. Nationalisme in de 3e wereld

12. Konvergentie en evolutie door Dr. J. van den Doel

DR. CH. BOASSON

Approaches to the Study of International Relations

WITH A FOREWORD BY PROF. DR. B. V. A. RÖLING

2nd. edition

VAN GORCUM & COMP. N.V. - ASSEN, 1972

ISBN 90 232 0923 0

Printed in the Netherlands by Royal Van Gorcum Ltd.

TABLE OF CONTENTS

FOREWORD BY PROF. DR. B. V. A. RÖLING

ACKNOWLEDGEMENTS

CHAPTER I — PHILOSOPHICAL PREFACE   p. 1
1. The Threat and its Perception   p. 1
2. Reconsidering some Difficulties   p. 2
3. Excluded Topics   p. 3
4. Raising Questions   p. 4
5. Questions and Master Keys   p. 5
6. Theory and Experience   p. 6
7. Looking Ahead   p. 6
8. Decision and Choice   p. 8
9. Theory and Utopia   p. 8

CHAPTER II — SOME THOUGHTS ON THEORY AND ON
INTERNATIONAL RELATIONS   p. 10
1. The Concept of Theory   p. 10
2. Divisions and Boundaries in Theory   p. 10
3. Problems and Tradition   p. 11
4. Problems in Contemporary Context   p. 12
5. Problems in other Fields of Interest   p. 13
6. Causal Fallacies   p. 15
7. Perspective: Imagination and Prediction   p. 16
8. Perspective: Ideals and Imagination   p. 18
9. Scientific Value Relativism   p. 19
10. A Community of Hope   p. 20

CHAPTER III — HISTORICAL RECONNAISSANCE   p. 22
1. Diplomatic History as the Story   p. 24
2. Diplomacy   p. 26
a. Diplomacy and Personal Recollection   p. 26
b. Diplomacy and Information   p. 28
c. Diplomacy and the Actors on the Scene   p. 29
d. Diplomacy and Political Behaviour   p. 32
e. Diplomacy and the Political Constellation   p. 34
3. Geography   p. 36
a. Geography and the Political Constellation   p. 36
b. Geography and Political Growth   p. 39
c. Geography and Human Endeavour   p. 40
d. Geography and Population Trends   p. 41

4. *History*   *p. 43*
a. History and Awareness   *p. 43*
b. History and Personalities or Trends   *p. 44*
c. History and Wisdom   *p. 46*
d. History and Prediction   *p. 48*

5. *Law*   *p. 50*
a. Law and the Origins of International Thinking   *p. 50*
b. Law: A World Community?   *p. 51*
c. Law and Integration of the Community   *p. 53*
d. Law and Membership of the Community   *p. 54*
e. Law and the Use of Force   *p. 55*
f. Law: Change and Self-Defence   *p. 56*

6. *Pacifism*   *p. 58*
a. Pacifism and Awareness   *p. 58*
b. Pacifism as a Propaganda   *p. 58*
c. Pacifism: Emotion and Planning   *p. 59*

CHAPTER IV — LATER ATTEMPTS AT A MORE EXHAUSTIVE
TREATMENT OF INTERNATIONAL
RELATIONS   *p. 61*

1. *Economics*   *p. 61*
a. Economics and Human Behaviour   *p. 61*
b. Economics and Sociology   *p. 63*
c. Economics and the Market-Concept   *p. 64*
d. Economics and the Market Fallacy   *p. 65*
e. Economics and a Plurality of Markets   *p. 66*
f. Economics and the Diversity of Markets   *p. 68*
g. Economics in Social Life   *p. 69*

2. *Politics*   *p. 71*
a. Politics and Human Behaviour   *p. 71*
b. Politics and Needs   *p. 73*
c. Politics and the International Scene   *p. 75*
d. Politics and Decision-Making   *p. 76*
e. Politics and Conflict   *p. 78*
f. Politics: Roles and Fears   *p. 79*
g. Politics and Systematic Analysis   *p. 81*
h. Politics and Expectations   *p. 82*
i. Politics and Improvement   *p. 83*
j. Politics and the Social Sciences   *p. 84*

3. *Sociology*   *p. 85*
a. Sociology leaves Gaps of Knowledge   *p. 85*

b. Sociology and Explanation p. 86
c. Sociology of Tensions p. 88
d. Sociology of Rational Conflict p. 88
e. Sociology: Population-Problems and Functionalism p. 90

CHAPTER V — NOTES ON METHODOLOGY p. 93

1. Lack of Disciplined Methodology p. 93
2. Simultaneous Problematics p. 94
3. Anxieties and Optimism Related to Methodology p. 95

CHAPTER VI — POSTSCRIPT p. 99

1. The Stream of Thought in Perspective p. 99
2. Peace Research p. 102
3. Strategic Thinking p. 104
4. International Communications p. 109
5. Quantitative International Politics p. 111
6. Simulation in International Relations p. 114
7. Animal Behaviour p. 115
8. Population and Ecology p. 117
9. Development p. 119

INDEX OF AUTHORS REFERRED TO p. 123

FOREWORD

What are the essential, driving forces in international relations? Is power the crux of the whole matter, as so many scholars want to suggest? And even if this be so, are the states driven by fear — has their power-politics a defensive character — or are they generally out on conquest — is their power-politics mainly aggressive? Do economic factors, whether or not in the open, play the decisive role? Or is it the situation in the world, the geophysical situation, which compels states to a specific foreign policy?

All kinds of factors can be mentioned, which, by one writer or another, are considered pivotal for the explanation of the attitude and the conduct of states in the world. The theory based on the generalisation of one such factor has often been, in its one-sidedness, an eye-opener for this special aspect of the problem. Such theories might therefore be considered as vital errors. They often lead to better insight than the sterile truths which, out of fear of error or partiality, contain only useless and paralysing generalities. Moreover, truth generally is more stimulating in its springtime of paradox than in its end-phase of platitude.

The Theory of International Relations is still in the phase of its vital errors. The theory of power and interest — generally adhered to by the present leading scholars — has served its main function: to put an end to the irrealistic 'idealism' of the inter-war period. In many theories of this 'twenty years crisis' it seemed as if in international relations morality and law formed the last word. The disappointment about the hypocrisy of that time brought to the for the almost cynical theory of power and interest, presented as the naked truth.

Meanwhile it is apparent, that the theory of power and interest might aim at quite different things. What kind of power is envisaged? Only military power, or also economic, moral or ideological power? And what kind of interest one has in mind? The direct, near and clear, tangible interest? Or the long-term interest, the enlightened interest, capable of taking into account the neighbor's interest, and compelled to forgo the short gain for the benefit of the long term?

Correctly one may assume that every living unit, including the national state, in its activity is focussed on its interests. That is a law of life, and probably the statesmen who preached the universal interest were mistrusted wisely. But at the heart of the matter lies the question of the measure in which the national interest is scanned in time and space. The question is in how far the circumstances (religious, spiritual, political, economic and technical) allow and compel the consideration of self-interest in the context of the whole world and in the light of the far future. That is a question of great complexity. To gain insight one needst to bring order in the subject-matter. Penetrating knowledge of the national group-life as well as of the international world is needed. The Theory of International Relations has to deal with the intern-national as well as with the international aspects.

In this study, Dr. Charles Boasson — whom, because of his active interest in its work and plans, the Polemological Institute likes to regard as a 'corresponding member' of its staff — tries interrogatively to create order in the chaotic whole of facts and theories. In his short survey of opinions and explanations the 'vital errors' are indicated and evaluated in their relative significance. As such, his study gives an important contribution to the creation of a general Theory of International Relations. As such, his study forms a constribution to the science of war and peace.

Polemology aims at learning to know the factors which play a role in the origin, and in the determination of the nature and the extent, of wars, and it endeavours to find the means which might restrict the occurence of war. To that end it is necessary to know more about the phenomenology of war, about its effects, about its functions and about its possible substitutes. Many, if not all sciences will have to contribute thereto, old sciences as History of Economy, new descilplines as Game Theory, Ecology, and Conflictology. It will be wellnigh impossible for the polemologist to evade the pitfalls of the onesided truths, the vital errors which, in an interplay of action and reaction, gradually approach reality. Historical insight may guard from unbearable theoretical one-sided-ness, and it may guarantee sousd and useful 'counsel to the Prince'.

War is a specific of international relations. Hence the intimate relations between Polemology and the Theory of International Relations. Polemology is, one might say, a chapter of the Theory of International Relations. This theory covers a wider field, not only the negative war-relations but also the positive peacerelations of co-operation. The Theory of International Relations, on the other hand, may be considered as a chapter of Polemology, which includes Conflictology, Game Theory, Theory of Strategy, Bargaining-theory and so many other general branches of science and learning.

The Study of Dr. Boasson is presented here as Volume II of the Polemological Studies, publications of the Polemological Institute at the University of Groningen. As a matter of course the responsibility for the contents of this study is the Author's.

B. V. A. RÖLING

ACKNOWLEDGEMENTS

Where I have consciously followed the ideas and expressions of others, I have tried to make my indebtedness explicit. However what I owe is greater than I could indicate in this way, for teachers, students and personal friends have all given the kind of help and encouragement which cannot be acknowledged in footnotes or bibliographies. As I cannot name them all I shall not name any of them, but my gratitude is great.

Having said this I must make one exception and thank Professor Vlekke, who initiated this paper. This is the third time he has invited me to prepare a paper for the Netherlands Society of International Relations and thus spurred me on to an effort which would not have been attempted without his initial encouragement nor continued without his unfailing guidance and patient discussion.

All the views expressed in this report are, of course, entirely my own, even where many of Professor Vlekke's suggestions have, I feel, resulted in improvements of my earlier draft.

This paper was prepared for the Netherlands Society of International Relations and submitted to the Society during the first half of 1962. During a later research assignment at the Department of International Law and Jurisprudence at the University of Sydney, I was able to benefit from suggestions of my Sydney colleagues both on style and technical handling. I wish to acknowledge this valuable help, as well as the generosity of the Research Committee of the University of Sydney in the facilities accorded to me.

CHAPTER I

PHILOSOPHICAL PREFACE

1. The Threat and its Perception

Viewpoints on International Relations are often preceded by threats of doom and tales of horror. Some writers believe that 'if we are to save ourselves' we should first of all 'be told what threatens us.'[1] Such 'shock-treatment' does not however guarantee the soundness of subsequent argument nor the certainty that then 'the whole weight of human wisdom'[2] in fact becomes available. The threat may be so overwhelming as to prevent us from reacting wisely and reasonably; cool and reasonable analysis moreover may fail to do full justice to the chaotic, tragic and weird implications of world affairs.

Discursive and dissective examination, the hall-mark of Western Scholarship, occasionally fails to convey to our mind how deep each single problem lies, how thoroughly interlocked the problems are and how necessary it is to consider them together rather than in isolation. This interdependence can often be indicated best by aphorism and illustration, as when the limitations of a possible thesis, 'peace through disarmament,' are indicated by an aphoristic reversal: 'Disarmament through Peace.'[3] This approach at least avoids the long-windedness which seem inevitable in many articulate theories of International Affairs and in some hands at least it can be suggestive and rewarding. But the dilemma is that 'articulateness and suggestiveness are, of course, incompatible.'[4] 'Aphorisms, allusions and illustrations are not articulate enough. Their insufficiency in articulateness is compensated for however by their suggestiveness.'[5]

---

[1] Wayland Young, *Strategy for Survival — First Steps in Nuclear Disarmament*, Harmondsworth, A Penguin Speciaal (1959) 86.
[2] *Id.* 87.
[3] B. H. M. Vlekke, 'Disarmament through Peace,' *NATO-Letter* vol. 9 No. 11 (November 1961).
[4] Fung Yu-lan (ed. D. Bodde), *A Short History of Chinese Philosophy*, New York, Mac-Millan (1948), Paperback ed. (1960) 12.
[5] *Ibid.*

In the hope of finding a remedy for these difficulties — namely a basic theoretical structure, more than one symposium has been dedicated to 'Grand' or 'Central' Theory. Indeed such collective efforts have produced invaluable fresh insights, yet very few models are generally accepted and there seems to be no 'agreed' theory nor a well deliminated field for the disciplined theoretical study of International Relations.[6]

2. Reconsidering some Difficulties

This paper will not so much attempt to join in the debate, not soon to be ended anyhow, as to what is proper 'theory' for the field, or what are hopeful suggestions; it will rather accept several approaches as fruitful and probably inevitable. It will not try to refute in lengthy arguments points of view which in my opinion are rejectable. The paper will reject such views without much ado. Only in cases where the rejected views seem extremely respectable in some circles or where the views seemed attractive at first and only proved untenable after further consideration (thus providing an important stimulation to fresh thinking) will a summary discussion, or at least some reference to such views, be given.

The paper will above all attempt to re-think what I believe to be admirable points of view, and in doing so to reconsider *difficulties* in the appreciation of acceptable and admissible theory. It will look for basic assumptions of accepted valuable thought which is worth re-thinking. Such re-thinking may, it is hoped, lead to a fruitful debate.

Such thought — including perhaps somewhat rather thoughtless experience — as can be said to fall within the 'theory' (or doctrine) of International Relations, will require special attention.[7] What is precisely covered by the 'field', ought not, thereafter, to detain us too much. In the abstract there is no occurrence and no idea, no way of living and no moral aspiration, no institution and no process which may or ought not to be related to the field.

[6] See, e.g. vol. IV. No. 3, *The Journal of Conflict Resolution* (Sept. 1960) or *Theoretical Aspects of International Relations* (ed. William T. R. Fox) University of Notre Dame Press (1959).
[7] See *infra* Ch. II.

3. Excluded Topics

However, two topics which often appear in the academic curriculum for International Relations will not be considered. The first of these is that aspect dealing with transactions and intercourse between nations, as exemplified in treaties, conferences, diplomatic representation and existing international agencies.

Often these topics are actually taken to cover the field exhaustively: in that case the 'field' is actually defined in a much too limited and rather easily surveyable sense. In any case that aspect of the field is already ably treated in various reference and text-books.[8] This little well-tended garden in spite of a possible chaotic corner here and there, will not be considered at all, unless more general conclusions must perhaps lead indirectly to a re-assessment of current assumptions on diplomacy and international contact. Certainly we shall have to test some assumptions on the *function* of diplomacy, a matter discussed *infra* Ch. III Section 2.

The other topic, similarly excluded, is the problem of educating students for the subject; the problem of creating faculties or enlarging and joining existing faculties. Excellent minds have given careful attention to the problem.[9] At the present stage of theoretical sophistication it might be disatrous if Universities were to attempt the replacement of the existing diversity of systems by some uniform pattern or were to aspire to integrate what *perhaps should not yet be considered integrable.*[10]

The educational problem involved nevertheless exerts additional

---

[8] Even students' books treat this sub-field adequately, e.g., L. Larry Leonard, *International Organization*, New York, MacGraw Hill (1951).
Stephen S. Goodspeed, *The Nature and Function of International Organization*, New York, Oxford University Press (1959).
[9] Grayson Kirk, *The Study of International Relations*, New York, Council on Foreign Relations (1947).
C. A. W. Manning, *The study of International Relations*, Paris, UNESCO, 1954.
C. Dale Fuller, *Training of Specialists in International Relations*, Washington D.C., American Council on Education (1957).
[10] An academic discipline too well integrated may smother fruitful and fresh ideas. How often have useful innovations not been contested bitterly by established universities?

pressures and demands for a straightforward teachable theory. The same problem may present itself again obliquely when educators reflect on the relation between theory and purpose or on the relation between theory and doubt: theory, as a rule, is born out of doubt.

The best training of students may then be above all the kind of training which carries doubt over into a systematically critial attitude and the basic benefit of Philosophy may, similarly, be found in the deliberative attitude it promotes. Indeed the greatness of some philosophers consisted exactly in this, that they could be disturbed by and could disturb others by questions which had not been asked, at least in that form, before.

4. Raising Questions

However the putting of just new odd questions is not enough: these must be related to the existing web of doctrine, or to similar, perhaps slumbering, questions weighing on other minds. The wanderings of a solitary mind usually become philosophically important only through the work of integrative interpretation, which shows how much apparently out-of-the-way questions are relevant to substantial problems of the (or of a later) day.

The greatness of philosophy, of scientific as well as of artistic work, consists mainly in the integrative craftmanship which relates the as yet unheard and unseen (or not thùs heard and thùs seen) to the already mastered.

It has been suggested that 'posing a central question and ordering systematically the different answers that can be given to it is the most direct route to the construction of international — political theory.'[11]

[11] Kenneth N. Waltz, 'Political Philosophy and the Study of International Relations' in *Theoretical Aspects of International Relations, op cit. supra* n. 6 at 62, cf. a review of this thesis in *World Politics* (Richard Snyder 'Some Recent Trends etc.') Vol. XIII: 2 (Jan. 1961) 300ff. at 305. Incidentally Waltz is not yet doing what he suggests in his article, but at the same time he is giving more by insisting that we must learn first from previous philosophers. He thereby adequately refutes, in my opinion, the earlier essay in the same study, Hans J. Morgenthau, 'The Nature and Limits of a Theory of International Relations' p. 15ff. which concentrates only on 'politics' and looks to the masterkey (admitting no other 'latch, or catch, or key') of 'power' and 'national interest.'

A symposium might readily attempt such a task . . . if the participants did not fundamentally disagree on what their 'field' was and on what might be a central question. This difficulty led to premature attempts to demark at least a 'field' to be agreed upon, so that the appropriate central questions might at once be, so to speak, 'planted'.

5. Questions and Master Keys

All the reports on such attempts towards an 'international theory' or towards 'Research for Peace'[12] tend to show that a well-defined field and a limited number of central questions cannot be agreed upon.

Why should it? Why, we should ask, this hurry, this impatience? True, the problems of International Relations and their urgency worry the serious student and researcher; however, worry should not lead to undue haste or to belief in master-keys. The mere belief in master-keys is already a tranquilizer; so is the belief that a neat theoretical conception of international relations will necessarily greatly assist the actor on the international scene.[13] It is not denied that such an actor often tries to 'justify' (at least as long as he is not yet the victim of self-idolization) his acts on the basis of his own theoretical insight; belief in the theoretical foundations behind one's action however, does not always prove the soundness of those foundations. The more cocksure the belief, the less it may prove. The medicinemen and surgeons in former times were possibly less hesitant in matters which the educated medical world of to-day, with its greater knowledge and its store of therapeutics, dare not treat with ready-made methods. It is not inconceivable that in an exceptional case a cocksure wonder-healer may obtain much better results than an undecided learned theoretician. The cocksureness may be the therapy!

It is also true that scope of learning does not yet make a good physician. It may well be that good physicians must shed off their scientific doubts at some stage of their medical performance — the stage where *experience completes theory*.

[12] Q. Wright, W. F. Cottrell and Ch. Boasson, *Research for Peace*, Amsterdam, North Holland Publishing Co. (1954).
[13] Hans Morgenthau, *op. cit. supra n.* 11, at 18, 21.

6. Theory and Experience

All this does not make theoretical foundation superfluous to the man of practice,[14] particularly where men of practice can rely on the satisfactory performances of their fore-runners. In that case the study of such past practice leads to satisfactory theory. Some politicians have in fact been learned and capable theoreticians. We would not regard it as a bad thing if political candidates the world over will be *required* to master a minimum of theoretical exercise before being let loose on the public at large. Since, however, past generations of political practitioners have not made such a good impression nor left the world better than it is, it seems that the theoreticians of international relations would themselves be well advised to go in for some further heart- and brain-searching about fundamental questions rather than considering themselves as backseat drivers to statesmen and diplomats. The more they try, prematurely, to limit the field to isolated clear-cut questions, the less they are likely to probe the full implications of their own theoretical foundation.[15] The more they try, on the other hand, to do justice to the complications, the ambivalences and uncertainties of problems waiting for a solution and confronting politicians, the less it can be said[16] that their theory assumes an unequivocal normative character.[17]

7. Looking Ahead

The desire to draw the blueprints for a normative and directive the-

---

[14] I hope to argue later that there is no such clear-cut distinction between good theory and good practice.

[15] A similar difficulty crops always up in theory: 'generality' covering a great variety of particular aspects may lose specific meaning (it gives merely an 'inkling' of insights); adequate treatment of 'specific' problems on the other hand differs from general theory (it gives 'full' insight, but into a tiny corner only).

[16] As Morgenthau implied, *op. cit. supra* n. 11 *ibid.*

[17] The present writer made an interesting experiment with fourth-term University students of 'Sociological Analysis in International Relations.' Several points brought up for discussion as 'debate of the month' in *Western World* were put before students. Those most advanced in their studies were least inclined to take a dogmatic stand and find an easy and certain solution.

ory of International Relations may stimulate too much the attempts to pose and consider central questions *whilst it is yet too early* to decide what questions are central or even whether *enough* questions have already been suggested. Each questioner poses questions *only in part* as a response to his own original doubts; in part he does so in continuation of, or under the inspiration of previously posed questions. A good and timely question fructifies research in that direction, but may divert scientific attention from directions where no inspiring questions have been asked, although they could and should have been asked or would, if asked, have been even more profitable.

General doubt-raising, with no specific central questions attached, may even more fructify International Relations theory. Much of this theory centers round problems of political decision-making or is simply equated with international politics[18] or this political corner of the field is defined as in some sense 'the nucleus' of the discipline.[19] This study will follow the fashion in this respect but not without the most serious qualsm about some of the assumptions which, during the last decades, have led to this particular 'political' stress.

There are, of course, reasons to welcome this closer attention to the political aspects. The evolution of this 'policy orientation'[19]a indicates at least an awareness and to some extent the direction of the re-orientated policies the world is in need of. This awareness is not limited to an intellectual exposition of the formal political structures of Society but covers the semi-rational influences of 'moods,' of prejudices and stereotypes[20]. To some extent methods were found to measure opinion, to classify types of opinion-makers, to relate the impact of opinion on decisions and, vice versa, to show the impact of a decision taken in defiance of pre-existing opinion.[21]

---

[18] Morgenthau, *op cit.* 15. Norman J. Padelford and George A. Lincoln, *International Politics*, New York, MacMillan, (1954) p. 4.

[19] Grayson Kirk, *The Study of International Relations in American Colleges and Universities*, New York. Council on Foreign Relations (1947) 10.

[19]a *The Policy Sciences* (Daniel Lerner and Harold D. Lasswell editors) Stanford University Press (1951).

[20] See *infra* Ch. IV, Section 2d.

[21] Karl W. Deutsch and Lewis J. Edinger in *Germany Rejoins the Powers,* Stanford University Press (1959) showed some interesting examples.

8. Decision and Choice

Nevertheless this stress on the 'political' has its dangers: in the first place the notion of the 'political' must be extended so as to refer back to economics, sociology and social science in general so that a precise meaning is lost (see hereafter Ch. IV, 2). The importance attached to 'decision-taking' may be greatly exaggerated and even the reverse may occur: a rational policy orientation may seem to the student of politics an utterly hopeless undertaking!

Occasionally it is difficult to distinguish between a decision of free choice and historically unavoidable necessity, between heroic action and the blind workings of fate.

This itself, apart from the delicate and hardly tractable problem of 'Scientific Value Relativism,'[22] makes it difficult to decide on a right course of action.

Scientific or let us say more 'detached' observers do not escape this predicament: their theoretical solutions seem either castles in the air or down-on-earth acceptance of the big bad world.

9. Theory and Utopia

If any basic assumption can help us at all in this apparent impasse, it is no doubt the assumption which is made by Stanley H. Hoffmann and formulated by him in a most concise — dangerously concise — but highly convincing manner[23]: in addition to systematic research, Hoffmann asserts, we are in need of 'relevant utopias'. Part of this paper will be an attempt to argue that the gulf between 'realist theory' and 'utopia' is not so wide as often believed, and is in part bridged by the use of 'models' or 'ideal types' in theory. Models and ideal types become more utopian where their relevancy has become remote. Many suggestions in international politics are utopian because based on irrelevant models. The model of 'law' for the international scene is, for example, taken from a cultural unit; that of 'government' from

[22] Probably the most thorough treatment of this problem in Arnold Brecht, *Political Theory*, Princeton University Press (1959).
[23] Stanley H. Hoffmann, *Contemporary Theory in International Relations*, Englewood Cliffs, Prentice Hall (1960) 184.

a historically grown and integrated community; or that of 'decency' from a group of persons who are fundamentally agreed on what they expect from life. On the other hand many suggestions are rejected out of hand as 'utopian' and unempirical without sufficient appreciation of their inherent desirability and their actual relatedness to empirically felt evils; evils which somehow *must* be removed, even if replaced by something less than the utopian solution prosposed. Utopian thinking, technical planning and ethical norm-giving are all related to the understanding of theory-formation in the Social Sciences. That being so, theory-formation must rely heavily on philosophic contemplation, if only for the purpose of testing and re-testing its own *relevancy* and *soundness*. Philosophic contemplation, however, is needed more in order to *reconsider* than to reject and, as suggested by Walter Kaufmann, when accepted tenets are criticized, this is not simply to 'choose between disturbing and offering something positive.'[24] The 'disturbing' element is rather the realization of how difficult positive suggestions are to attain.

[24] Walter Kaufmann, *Critique of Religion and Philosophy*, London, Faber & Faber (1959) XIV.

CHAPTER II

SOME THOUGHTS ON THEORY AND ON INTERNATIONAL RELATIONS

1. The Concept of Theory

The word 'theory' is derived from 'to look at,' to 'conceive.' Any intellectual look at a situation, any situation, can be called 'theorizing.' If really no trouble is aroused by the situation, there will be very little theory indeed. A slight difficulty in a situation will cause most of us to stop acting for a moment and to engage — perhaps only for the fraction of a second — in thinking. When we can continue our action, after that intellectual suspension-of-breath, we have found 'good' theory. When we can not, we are in need of theory. Yet, often we continue in the old way although we should have changed our line of action: we were in need of theory but not aware of it. 'Insight in a flash' only becomes theory in the more normal usage of the word when 'remembered' and 'organized'. A remembered solution leads or can lead, at a later stage, to a repeat-performance.

2. Divisions and Boundaries in Theory

In order to handle a situation intellectually we usually carve up the totality of the situation into more manageable units. After that we reconstruct again into a whole those separate details which have become disconnected in the process of our own analysis. Theorizing is both dividing entities and combining divided parts. We cannot always fully realize in advance the implications of the division made, the frontiers drawn, and we may well become the victim of our exaggerated belief in the reality and survival value of such arbitrary divisions and frontiers. Especially when dealing with the geographic focus in international situations, when comparing physical units with social units, this difficulty is obvious. However, this theoretical difficulty pervades all aspects of International Relations: boundaries and divisions are made to comprehend situations. The 'field' of study by any definition transcends the very boundaries with which we are confronted.

It is not only the drawing of boundaries, however, which may be misleading but also the combinations which we make. 'Expert' theory may derive from experience (just repeat-performance after trial and error) or from keen intellectual reflection and contemplation, or from deep abstract and anticipatory thinking. A 'litte' theory is not more than a first stepping stone to expert theory: quantitative and qualitative handling of the situation (or, handling in the abstract, which is called also 'in theory') is likely to lead from such little theory to more fundamental expert theory.

The more 'expert' a theory the more it should cover a whole series of problems and the more it must explain apparently hidden interrelationships. For that reason expert theory, although growing through experience or through substantial intellectual effort out of little theory, may yet be more basically mistaken than superficial theory.

3. Problems and Tradition

Many contemporary problems were covered by earlier theoreticians.[25] In the meantime however many subproblems have shifted; not always so much in regard to fundamentals as in their scope and implications. When one thinks of giant national states and not any more of small city-states; of modern means of communications and transport and no more of messengers on horseback; of radio-propaganda instead of circulating pamphlets: then the quantitative shift may take on qualitative proportions. The similar has already become dissimilar.

In the old days the stage-coach and the canal-boat were means of communication in more than one respect, but fast planes and overcrowded publec vehicles are powerful means of *isolation* as well as of communication. The same applies in many respects to television.

Theories covering the 'Field' in former days, whether presented by philosophers, historians, lawyers or otherwise, may already have been somewhat defective in the beginning (in so far as they were contradictory, some of them must have been). The possibly irrelevant mi-

[25] See *infra* Ch. III.

nors errors of those earlier days may by now have become fatal mistakes, when applied to modern conditions. Nevertheless 'theoretical doctrine' is always to a great extent wisdom and reflection on an earlier problem applied to a *later* one. For the very reason that 'doctrine' is the total remembered and organized reflective thought in a certain field, it continues in a historical line and is therefore conditioned by thinking of the past.

Where past thinking has been unable to comprehend the existence of a problem or to forsee the appearance of one, then the later theory will err in so far it accepts the problems of the past as central and belittles or neglects problems which were overlooked or were non-existent before.

4. Problems in Contemporary Context

If our contemplation is influenced by past masters of thought, we also adapt past contemplation to our own nature, to the distortions of our own mind and to the prevailing opinions in our surroundings.

A standard volume of readings in social psychology[26] devotes a chapter to the phenomena of 'memory, judgment, perception, motivation as influenced by social conditions' and in fact, the main concern of social psychology is the study of the influence of prevailing group-opinion on the individual members of the group.[27]

While then we are in one way dominated by problems of the past, in another we appreciate these problems and their theoretical description and analysis under the influence of what are, according to our environment, the problems of the day. Our thoughts, even whilst aspiring to the realistic and objective, are moulded by 'past' frames of reference and by 'group' frames of reference.

---

[26] Theodore M. Newcomb, Eugene L. Hartley *et al*, *Readings in Social Psychology* New York, Henry Holt & Co. (1947) 69-129.

[27] Pioneers in this research were: Muzafer Sherif, *The Psychology of Social Norms*, Harper & Bros, New York, (1936).

Kurt Lewin, 'Frontiers in Group Dynamics' (1947) vol. I, *Human Relations*, 2-38.

Gardner Murphy, *Personality, A Biosocial Approach*, New York, Harper & Bros. (1947), and in the International Relations field the two authors hereafter mentioned.

The group-reference may be a degraded uncritical belief in what is accepted by others. But is need not be so, for in some groups appreciation goes to independent thinkers and in any case it is true that 'no man is an island,' not even in his efforts to arrive at a free and well considered judgment.

In the field of International Relations one of the most fertile thinkers in a very thoughtful book speaks of the 'Reference Group Hypothesis,' according to which 'we should expect to find a connection between an individual's attitude towards foreign affairs and the specific standards and norms dominant in the groups to which the individual relates himself.'[28] This of course is important when we think of the development of international attitudes,[29] but also when we reflet on the development of theory. While an acute awareness of this will not isolate us from the basic assumptions and conceptions of our environment or working group, it will perhaps better enable us to avoid dogmatising these assumptions into infallible starting points.[30]

5. Problems in other Fields of Interest

Fruitful development of theory takes place by relating problems in one situation not only to problems in a similar situation, but to other situations generally. Fructifying comparisons are not limited to a narrow field: theory development in all kinds of scientific fields is interrelated.

Sometimes dangerous imitations occur because scientist in one field are over-impressed by results of theory in other fields and try to adapt such successful theory to the problems of their own field. The dangers are many: the adaptors may have no deep understanding of the theory in the other field (they may indeed misconstrue it completely); the admired theory of that other field may perhaps have be-

---

[28] Bjørn Christiansen, *Attitudes towards Foreign Affair as a Function of Personality,* Oslo University Press (1959) 77.
[29] L. Queener, *Journal of Social Psychology* Vol. 29 (1947) 221-252 and Vol. 30 (1947) 105-126.
[30] The 'Sociology of Knowledge' proposed by Karl Mannheim, *Ideology and Utopia* (1927), New York, Harcourt, Brace & Co. (1936) probably overestimates greatly the possibility of 'escaping' from the group-reference. See *infra* Ch. IV, 3 c.

come obsolete; or it may be basically inappropriate to the field into which it is being introduced.

Social scientists have sinned heavily in trying to use mathematical theory or the thinking of the physical sciences indiscriminately in dealing with social phenomena, without probing into the applicability of such theory or its appropriate adaption to the social field. The most serious derailments in this respect have been reliance on 'regularity' in social occurrences long after the philosophy of physical and chemical sciences was already paying attention to unstable situations and to the pitfalls of 'regular-ness'. Social — particularly legal — scientist often refer to 'causality' or to 'logical relationships' in a sense which has long been abandoned by physicists or logicians.[31] On account of the substantial amount of both mathematical and philosophical training required, much sociological work, particularly 'social planning,' is set up by some scientists who have to rely on mathematicians for most of the reasoning involved. Many social scientists came from the 'humanities' in the first place but even those who had elementary training in mathematics and statistical methods have usually little or no training in the philosophical logic of the mathematics of chance, estimation, information and what one of the greatest experts in this field has called 'the underworld of probability.'[32]

On the other hand the enormous advance in mathematical social theory, the careful use of models and scales,[33] has not rendered less precise speculative thought entirely superfluous, although attempts to combine the two need great care and awareness. Mathematics and statistics can establish that specific characteristics of certain persons are likely to cause or promote a particular situation, or inversely, that a

[31] When Hans Kelsen is using and stressing the word 'logical' in his *General Theory of Law and State,* Harvard University Press (1945) XV, 440, he is using 'logic' in the sense of ancient logicians, perhaps referring merely to the 'ana-logic' element in logic. It is not at all difficult to refute Kelsen's fallacy but it requires some patience. See Julius Stone, *The Province and Function of Law,* Sydney, Associated General Publication (1946) and Ch. Boasson, *Sociological Aspect of Law and International Adjustment,* Amsterdam, North Holland Publishing Co. (1950).

[32] Ronald A. Fisher, *Statistical Methods and Scientific Inference,* Edinburg, Oliver and Boyd (2 ed. 1959).

[33] Paul F. Lazarsfeld (ed.), *Mathematical Thinking in the Social Sciences,* Glencoe, The Free Press (1954).

particular situation evokes or brings certain characteristics (which may have been latent) to the fore amongst participants in the situation.[34] But what are the *initial* formative factors leading to a particular social atmosphere? What are the chances of development at a starting point where no substantial information is yet available? In part our problem will be very speculative; in part our decisions will be influenced anyhow by ideas of a moral obligation, of an 'ought' (See infra sub. 8) where mathematical argument does not count for much — not even for well-trained mathematicians.

Some social scientists adopt mathematical argumentation in their thinking, with no awareness of the fundamental doubts which an appropriate mathematical approach would leave room for, and without feeling that the mathematics of social phenomena are *not* the primitive mathematics taught at secondary schools.

6. Causal Fallacies

The relationships which our mind desires to establish between events can sometimes be refined by mathematical formulation, but to some extent mathematical handling necessarily leaves intact the original set-up, the original mental picture: when the data into the mathematical formula were *incorrect,* they are not 'purified' by the procedure, although occasionally incorrectness may come to light. When the substantive data were at the outset *insufficient,* there is no mathematical remedy, although correct mathematical formulation may diminish the amount of data required for relevant fact-finding or may demonstrate that conclusions are not warranted. Without mathematical checking we might have prematurely jumped to conclusions by intuition, or have been misled by too small a number of similar occurrences. Not all mathematical formulation, however, includes adequate mathematical checks. 'Correlations' statistically found, on a correct mathematical basis, do not guarantee moreover that there may not be *multiple* correlations or over-determinedness. And even a single 'cor-

[34] E.g., The Newcomb experiment in Bennington College supports the thesis of a mutual re-inforcement where a liberal, tolerant atmosphere influences newcomers and at the same time the attitudes of the teaching staff and oldtimers establish the atmosphere.

relation' and complete determinedness (if a — then b; if b — than a) between two phenomena does not amount to a 'causal' explanation.

Non-mathematical representation in our minds is apt to run ahead of theory. Indeed without such surreptitious 'pre'-concluding not much expansion of theory would take place at all! But, especially in the social sciences, *checking* of unwarranted theoretical ('preconcluded') thinking is extremely difficult. The intuitive 'advancepictures' are complex and vague at the same time. Three pictures are likely to be confusedly present in our mind before we form the more crystallized conception of any event. That is to say, we look, figuratively speaking, at at least three levels of reflection aroused by our observation. Firstly: we picture some 'causal' or 'creative' factors which led to the event and which are inherent in it (whereby we judge as if everything must have *a cause* and *is itself a cause in a chain of events*). Secondly: we conceive also something like the future shape of the observed thing (as we expect it to bevome) and thirdly: we picture something like `the *ideal* shape of the thing observed (as we would *like* or *require* it to be in perfect form). All these back-ground aspects of the phenomenon observed (its assumed past, its future type as well as its 'ideal type') greatly influence the observation and conception we form of the supposedly objective 'fact' concerned. They all have a 'mental-optical' relevance.

7. Perspective: Imagination and Prediction

The imaginative perception of (or mental 'jump' toward) the likely future shape of an observed phenomenon has the greatest scientific value; it can be better guided than the other 'jumps', for it can be better checked and when the checking proves it to have been abortive we are more willing (though this is not always certain) to change our mind. Some scientists indeed take the position that prediction is the only hall-mark of science and that what is not rendered predictable, is not even treated scientifically. Those scientists do, of course, not exclude from science 'fields' where prediction is extremely difficult or where alternative possibilities have even chances. They insist however that such difficult prediction-problems be broken up into smaller units so that prediction becomes possible or the 'evenness' of the chances can be demonstrated.

Yet, in general, it seems that theory which attempts the elucidation of relationships or the suggestion of ideal types can also be handled in a scientific or at least reasonable atmosphere. For the time being in any case it seems as if the theory of International Relations will be more concerned with explanation and with the construction of 'relevant utopias' (see supra Ch. I) than with prediction. Strangely enough most social scientists seem to assume that the natural sciences are 'explaining' sciences par excellence and that they are successful in prediction precisely for that reason. It is much more likely however that the natural sciences have become so efficient in explaining natural phenomena 'backwards' for the opposite reason: namely because *predictive* thinking — foreseeing future events evolving from present observation — is so much easier feasible and controlable in natural than in social occurrences.[35] Let us not forget that we judge 'explanation' by a mixture of 'reasonableness' and 'predictive adequacy' and that neither provides fool-proof evidence for the correctness of the explanation.[36]

As I have said before, our observation is 'coloured' by conceptions of a past leading up historically or causally (although this is often anthropomorphic causality only, really a superstituous belief in causality) to the present and by the conception of a likely (probable) future *and* by a third conception of a desirable, an 'ideal', future. The idea of the past, the historical 'prior,' we in fact form *backwards*. We do not start from innocence and ignorance and observe it directly. Rather do we see it parlty through the eyes of other people who have put *their* conception of that past to book, and partly through our own

---

[35] In physical sciences moreover the chain of events can be easier subdivided; the 'ideal type' situation is — and *can* be so — less charged with ethical and traditional considereation, and the 'ideal type' situation can also be more easily conceived in an abstract form more nearly approximating to correctness. For even if we could change our 'ideal' images in social situations with somewhat greater ease (as we apparently can in physical imagination, although there too we have restraints) we have much less guarantee that the *ideal* image is *relevant* than in physical theorizing, where checking and isolating are so often possible, and where multi-correlatedness can be traced much more easily and then broken up or discounted.
[36] On the nature of sociological explantion see *infra* Ch. IV, Section 3b.

eyes which always see the present *first*, even though this seeing of the present is in itself influenced by how others saw (and we see) the past. In the social world this adapting of the past *and* present to a fitting whole (figuratively speaking: this adapting of the several 'foci' to a confluent whole) leads more easily to distortions than in the physical world, although even there we make optic mistakes, assuming that things probably were as they appear now or that change in our time has been preceded by similar and *continuous* change. Moreover, the concepts of the past, present and the two futures (the probable as against the ideal) are always 'extracts' only, enormous simplifications. The 'probable-future-concept' we can check only if we have time to live to see our prediction come either true or false; provided moreover we have been precise enough in our predictive image and in the later observation to be able to say really whether the prediction was true or false. Some vagueness in either the earlier image or in the later observation may prevent this clear cut 'either — or'.

Certainly in respect of our projections backwards into the past we can not help seeing the present so much 'first', that recent experiences and historical documentation really interweave. For example, some historians have drawn portraits (probably caricatures) of Napoleon influenced by their observation of 20th century dictators[37] and which have not taken adequate account of the fact that what happened later was not appreciated thèn at all. We can practically never say with certitude that what happened later was already then rigidly predestined,[38] something which occasionally can be said in physical experiment.

8. Perspective: Ideals and Imagination

The question which has vexed social scientists, and which can not be evaded in International Relations theory any more than in Political Theory, is the relation between our conception of the present and the

---

[37] J. Presser, *Napoleon*, Amsterdam, Elsevier (1946) is one of them. Why was J. L. Talmon's *The Origins of Totalitarian Democracy*, London, M. Secker and Warburg (1952) not titled: 'The *possible* origins etc.'...? (as it might have been if written only twenty years before!)

[38] Isaiah Berlin, *Historical Inevitability*, Oxford University Press (1954), makes a passionately reasoned plea against historical determination.

probable on one hand and our conception of the desirable and ideal on the other. It is *not* enough to distinguish between the *is* and the *ought,* nor to emphasize that the *ought* can not be explained or established by the *is.* There seem to be more and more voices, saying that the *is* of a social fabric or a social process should not be analyzed without at least some inkling of the 'oughts' valid within (or for) that fabric and that process.

It would be a vain hope, in this brief theoretical prelude, to delve deeply into one of the most vexing and baffling aspects of social philosophy. Yet a working suggestion may be attempted on these lines:

The pre-scientific contemplation of any social occurence is profoundly influenced by the fact that we regard some occurrences from several points of view, and these points of view or foci are themselves not mutually exclusive or independent but function simultaneously. It is impossible to separate sharply the historical, quasi-explanatory, way of looking; the concern with evaluating possible and probable developments; and the moral concern with relating the occurrence to the ideal and the desirable. These conceptual foci are present in practically *all* members of society though of course their degree of refinement varies greatly from person to person. The concepts around each focus, however, are only partly developed as a result of scientific analysis on a high level (this analyzing influence may be insignificant, or much less significant than some scientists would like to admit) and their development largely follows uncontrollable 'moods,' 'fashions' or other casual trends.

It is important to acknowledge however that scientific — tolerant, searching, philosophical and logical — discussion of all these concepts and of their interrelationship, is to some extent possible — that indeed such a discussion will be the most obvious way of developing social theory.

9. Scientific Value Relativism

Much that has been said on social phenomena such as law, ethics, national character and so forth will not fit in with the point of view, defended here, where the 'is' and the 'ought' are not so radically severed. Instead of a simplistic abyss between the 'is' and the 'ought' it seems more fruitful to compare the development of these phenomena with stages in economic planning. What has grown (the 'is') in the economic sphere and what is set as a target (the 'ought') are also interrelated.

This assumption (of some relationship between the 'is' and the 'ought') denies that there exist moral absolutes, valid everywhere, *a priori;* accordingly, when such an *a priori* moral imperative is nevertheless felt (as it *must* be felt before an ethical decision can be taken) the ethical norm is not assumed to be unerringly obtainable by scientific approach.

This is plain 'Scienitfic Value Relativism',[39] which admits the plurality of value systems, denies the possibility of establishing an 'order' or hierarchy among moral or religious concepts by scientific means and knows not how to link scientific or reasonable discussion with the capacity to take a moral decision. This is not to deny that some overriding common moral values may be found in practically every society, even if under the disguise of a very varied cultural relativity.[40] In spite of scientific investigation, however, some ethical 'indeterminacy will always remain.'[41]

Possibly there is a bridge between the two — science and morality — namely *alertness,* the overcoming of laziness and prejudice.

If there are philosophic bridges between knowledge and morality they are certainly not bridges which have been built once and dor all by others on whom responsibility can be thrown.

10. A Community of Hope

When basic assumptions give no definite ranking order in moral goodness, some of the arguments against the wickedness of rulers may fail to convince. It need not be denied that some rulers succeeded in

[39] See Arnold Brecht, *op. cit. supra,* n. 22, *passim.*
[40] This is a view akin to that of Theodore M. Greene, 'Secular Values and Religious Faith' in A. Dudley Ward (ed.) *Goals of Economic Life,* New York, Harper & Bros. (1953) 371ff. Yet I do not share Greene's over-evolutionist hopes; and instead of his belief in the 'apprehensibility' of 'embodied values,' I prefer to speak of tolerant discussion.
[41] Abraham Edel, *Ethical Judgment,* Glencoe, 'The Free Press' (1955) 336 and *passim.*

wielding political power because they were criminals and that some others became criminal because their own power overwhelmed them. Admittedly this is a problem in International Relations Theory. A much greater problem, however, arises where rulers and their subjects have been in conflict with each other, not as a result of simply criminal inclination but in perfectly good faith.[42]

When on the other hand we admit that no ever-valid moral ranking order can be established, we must ponder, whether we do not destroy the possibility of discussion with most true-believers or — worse — destroy the possibility of ultimate hope altogether. Against this it must be observed that relativists ought at least to desire continued discussion with all 'believers' who are not too rigid to condescend to such plane of discussion; possibly much of the destruction is really begun on the believer's side. Belief in revelation, it seems, may be of two kinds: one a narrow belief in salvation not to be shared with anyone not professing identical 'grace'; another serving as a point of safety and consolation not preventing ventures into fields of doubt, where security-risks inherent in empiricism, logical argument and indefinite answers are met.

Some religious thinkers feel themselves engaged in an unfinished debate between themselves ('I') and Infinity ('Thou').[43] It is difficult to say that religious search and anxiety are more sincere when partaken in by those who stipulate blank passivity (such as sometimes Karl Barth may seem to imply) than they are when the participants are those who admit some 'prior understanding,' who admit that 'one must have *some*[44] experience and notion (however implicit) of good and evil, of death, of guilt and forgiveness, before the word of Revelation can be heard and understood.'[45] It is submitted that between this second group of believers and the relativist (some of whom are perhaps a 'latent' kind of believer) there exist bridges of communication and a community of hope.

---

[42] See *infra* Ch. IV, 3.
[43] Martin Buber is a conspicuous adherent of this school of thought and has made it perhaps more articulate than ever before.
[44] Italics not in the original.
[45] Fred Berthold Jr., *The Fear of God*, New York, Harper & Bros., (1959), 109. In the original Berthold wrote 'the Gospel' where I have substituted 'Revelation.'

CHAPTER III

HISTORICAL RECONNAISSANCE

Many topics which various scientists have analyzed during the last decades had already been studied and discussed by previous generations. We may assert without too much exaggeration that earlier thinkers often saw their field (history, geography, diplomacy, law) as including and exhausting the whole subject of International Relations. Only when those with an historical approach gradually felt the need of a geographic or legal approach in addition to their own, did International Relations begin to emerge as a specific 'field.' This emergence of a new field grew out of the awareness of the *insufficiency* of the monodisciplinary approach and not because that discipline (as *sole* approach now insufficient) had lost all relevance or should be abandoned altogether. This is occasionally lost sight of.

Scientists in the later developed branches of social science, such as social psychology, sociology, economics and political science, did — usually on the basis of their aspirations to cover the whole of social life — set aside a *corner* for International Relations. The latecomers' approach has therefore its own obvious dangers: in the first place this hole-in-the-corner attention to international affairs as part of social-life-in-general has very often been hurried, sloppy and by way of a sort of 'concluding' or 'summarizing' thought on the part of the modern social scientist. This even applies, and in such case is more serious than when the sinner is a superficial writer by nature, to first-rate and painstaking authors in their field. It seems as if these accurate and careful authors say, when having reached the end of their argument: 'see, this is what happened in the development of national government, or of national solidarity-feeling and don't worry too much about the crashes from international disturbances, because *eventually* the development on a world scale will follow (necessarily!) the development from scattered social communities to large national or even federal entities.' This is the danger of hurry, of the hole-in-the-corner (instead of central) treatment, and of assuming forever similar, continuous growth. In addition it is the sort of conclusion which can only be reached by a very superficial study of history, since it ignores the fact that the disintegration of large political units has been as characteristic a feature of this century as has the consolidation of small ones.

Another danger is the exaggerated importance attached to the latecomers' approach by its adepts. Often this approach has been chosen by the scientist *in despair of* the old-time professions. The historian, especially the student of diplomatic history who has come to discover the shortcomings of his study, turns with his messianic hopes to political science, the international lawyer to sociology or the geographer to social psychology. The earlier disciplines seem to have bristled with 'utopians' and 'believers,' and the converted latecomers may either transplant their (usually irrelevant!) utopian expectations to a new and modern science of social life or approach the new disciplines as 'dismal sciences,' approaches suitable to their disillusions. As Maxwell Cohen[46] has eloquently put it: 'A social scientist is so often a frustrated lawyer!'.

These 'frustrated' students from the old time branches of Social Science will normally not put International Relations into a 'corner' of their newly guided attention, but — the other way round — they will adapt the study of the theory of International Relations to the method of their newly embraced science and to that method *only*.

If the old-timers seemed to have a somewhat mono-maniac faith in their field of study because of a lack of experience, the latecomers tend to develop a monomaniacal faith in their new discipline because of the bitter taste of their former experience. It is emphatically submitted that theory-formation in International Relations must advance slowly, that too much search for a new original discipline is as misleading as uncritical acceptance of the assumptions and metods of the oldtimers. Turning now first of all to some of the more 'classical' approaches to International Relations I will try to discover at least some of the basic assumptions contained in these.

---

[46] In a lecture, not published.

I. Diplomatic History as the Story

The first approach which certainly has not died out in our generation, is that which seeks to arrive at a theoretical treatment of International Relations through description, usually description of diplomatic-military history. Diplomatic-military history is that particular historical analysis which is frequently identified with International Relations. It is claimed that in the same way that it is possible to study the history of a town, of a family, of an art or of an idea, it is also possible to exhaust International Relations by describing diplomatic and military activity. Description of past events must of course aspire to a level far above the collection of curiosities and anecdotes. It becomes 'theory' because it selects according to given principles and draws conclusions.

A fairly recent example of such an historical approach which throws light on the whole method is provided by E.H. Carr. An historian and former official of the British Foreign Office, Professor Carr actually gave his historical survey of the period 1918-1939 the title *International Relations Between the Two World Wars*[47] and described it as an attempt at 'stocktaking' (though in fact another of his books with a more explicitly 'historical' title — *The Twenty Years Crisis*[48] — could be more accurately described as such an attempt). Obviously Professor Carr's analytical-historical sketches are but part of a long, long tradition, and some equally relevant examples or, for the purpose of obtaining a really 'pure' sample of the *genre*, some even better examples could be easily obtained from the body of work it has produced. Yet the very 'impurity' of Carr's work in this sense, the fact that he does not push reliance on official, *ex cathedra* statements of governments and politicians to the point of absurdity, that he is much

---

[47] E. H. Carr, *International Relations Between the Two World Wars*, London, MacMillan (1947).

[48] E. H. Carr, *The Twenty Years Crisis*, London, MacMillan (1939). This book has perhaps never been more adequately 'placed' than by William T. R. Fox in his 'The Uses of International Relations Theory' in *Theoretical Aspects of International Relations*, op cit. supra n. 6, 29, 30. The present writer must admit that, before considering afresh what Prof. Fox has said, he had not succeeded in abstracting Carr's book from the appeasement debate; it came to his bookshelf too early.

more than a compiler of available statements, that he consciously and explicitly searches for a sound theoretical foundation, and that he combines the qualities of a one-time official expert with those of a man of broad general culture, save his historical-reflective method from becoming a caricature and make it a more interesting example to consider. There have been less prudent authors in the same vein who seemed to risk saying that all wisdom and cross-cultural insights must be distilled from the historical sketch.

An eminent scholar such as Raymond Aron,[49] who should certainly be classified alongside E. H. Carr as being amongst the best representatives of the historical approach has moreover stressed the *impossibility* of drawing any sensible conclusion at all in International Relations *without at least* a thorough socio-historical investigation. Perhaps it is possible to render the basic assumption of this approach somewhat popularly as follows: 'no abstract wisdom will tell you anything in International Relations unless you first arrange your raw material, your events, in historical order.'

The 'theory,' in this approach is thus, as said, not in the events, but in the analytical arrangement. In the words of Aron: 'The mere story of events teaches us nothing unless it is given form and meaning by references to concepts; unless it entails an effort to distinguish the essential from the subsidiary.' Obviously no international-historian wants to remain a story-teller; his object is 'stock-taking'. But stock-taking as viewed 'against the background of the historical political complex,'[50] not as viewed against a broad spectrum of general scientific concepts. True, you can not be a wise historian without an inkling of psychology, geography or any of the other more recent sciences. This approach, however, sets the historical *ordering of events* first and concept-formation, when not serving this purpose, or rather when not a servant of this order, is rejected. However, even if the learning from *other* disciplines was extended without limits, nothing would be gained by this approach, the end result would still remain anecdotical story telling, only on an immensely wide front. When, however, all concept-formation is intended to become historically 'in-

[49] Raymond Aron, 'Conflict and War from the Viewpoint of Historical Sociology,' in R. Aron *et al* (ed.), *The Nature of Conflict*, Paris, UNESCO (1957), 177-203.
[50] Aron, *id*, 185.

formative'[51] a disquieting question arises: This approach, which has emphatically been and perhaps still is the most used, the most obvious approach and which has not always been used with the subtlety, alertness and awareness shown by Carr and Aron, actually asserts that the reflection on historical experience is sufficient theory. Is this true?

We are all under a great obligation to those who enable us to grasp or regrasp events (or 'essentials') of the past. We can agree with them that we are in need of an awareness — in essentials — of that past. And yet, to the very extent that we catch again the 'reality' of the past, must not we also *escape* its grasp, placing the reality and its former *alternatives* above all in a larger frame? Do we not become 'wise' historians to the extent that in fact we have turned to other disciplines instead of to historical reproductive correctness or essentialism? Says Aron:[52] 'only a sociologist using the historical method could become the Adviser of the Prince.' But is a good Chronicler per sé a good Adviser? Is not the road from chronicle to advice anti-historical in a sense? There are surely limits to the application of such an aphorism as 'good advice is the clever reading of history in reverse.' Is putting the Chronicler in the shoes of an Adviser not *hurried wishful thinking*, an impatience which may in itself impair the accuracy of the Chronicler?[53]

2. Diplomacy

a. Diplomacy and Personal Recollection. The description of 'Diplomatic and Military History,' selective as it has always been, did as a rule mirror (with a long time-lag) actual diplomatic intercourse — the kind of bargaining, intrigue and personal relationships which found final expression in wishes, regrets and demands.

Diplomacy is an old profession and no one engaged in it has ever been much inclined to take a lowly view of his activities. It seems moreover that the temptation to write 'memoirs', and to picture in

[51] Aron, *id.* 185; on historical 'information' generally see: *infra* Ch. III, 4.
[52] *Id.* 203.
[53] When returning in Ch. III, Section 4 to the science of history (as a total science, not as 'international' history) still other aspects of the inconclusiveness of historical wisdom will confront us.

those memoirs the transactions of the diplomatic profession as decisive for the fate of nations and of the world were hazards of the profession. The descriptive efforts in this field usually fall short of the more exact and plain 'diplomatic and military history' by historically trained scientists. The memoirs of diplomats are nevertheless considered most important raw material which might divulge as yet secret and spicy aspects of the game, aspects which were available to the statesmen and their representatives only, and *not* to the learned commentator, however up to date 'historically.' Yet, occasionally, we may suddenly find the opposite: rulers or even responsible cabinet-ministers may have arrived at conclusions and attitudes of which their own diplomatic envoys are *purposely* kept ignorant.[54] Admitting that diplomats are probably up to date on 'confidential' matters, there still remains a great problem as to their 'intake' from a position of close, often friendly, contact with the Great and Mighty. They often and notoriously lack contact with upsurging new-comers, especially in conditions of sudden and violent change.

In the long run diplomatic memoirs, even when they may contain secret and confidential items may amount to little more than interesting collections of curiosities which lack any understanding of the basic forces in world events.

Recent fundamental thinking on diplomatic activity has tended to stress this and a chapter is devoted to it in the substantial Report on U.S. Foreign Policy by the U.S. Senate Committee.[55] This awareness has been particularly stimulated by the Massachusetts Institute of Technology with its great stress on the analysis of 'communicative activity',[56] and of 'modernization' in traditional patters of living.[57] This

[54] The problem is discussed by Jacques de Bourbon-Busset in his article (77ff., esp. 83); 'Decision Making in Foreign Policy' in Stephen D. Kertesz and M. A. Fitz Simmons (eds.), *Diplomacy in a Changing Word*, University of Notre Dame Press (1959).

[55] U.S. Foreign Policy Committee on Foreign Relations (2 vols.) *Report to 86th Congress 2nd Session*, 1186ff. (September 1960).

[56] Karl W. Deutsch, *Nationalism and Social Communication*, New York, Massachusetts Institute of Technology and John Willy & Sons (1953).

[57] Daniel Lerner *et al*, *The Passing of Traditional Society, Modernizing the Middle East*, sponsored jointly by the Massachusetts Institute and Columbia University, Glencoe, Free Press (1958).

raises a point as to the selection and education of 'experts' in international relations who can be 'the eyes, ears and voice'[58] of their country in the countries to which they are assigned. Whilst this is not, as I have said before, our problem, we must touch upon the assumption, perhaps it is better to say the traditionality of the assumption, of the overriding importance of diplomatic representation if combined with the diplomat's ability to (a) sense and obtain important information, (b) watch over and defend the dignity and enhance the respect of his native state and (c) struggle for favourable position or advancement through 'diplomatic ability'.

All these assumed necessities and possibilities colour the theoretical importance attached to diplomacy in International Relations.

b. Diplomacy and Information. The times have long gone when hardly any information could be gained on other states if not through diplomats and their staff. With the possibility of scanning newspapers, scientific, commercial and statistical publications, of listening to broadcasts etc., it is practically as convenient to concentrate the largest part of information-gathering in the research departments of a Foreign Ministry as to rely on information-gathering under the direction of a diplomatic representative, who spends so many hours of the day in just representing. The romantic days are also gone when militairy information of the greatest importance could only be obtained by a 'beautiful but dangerous woman, necessarily a brunette' appearing in unexpected places or even moving 'through the Balkan night on the gaily lighted Orient Express.'[59]

If the U.S. Senate Committee Report on Foreign Policy informs us that there are two thousand civilian employees of the U.S. foreign services in the United Kingdom alone, part of whom no doubt are specializing in the intake of facts, not secret facts but facts ready to be learned openly if one knows how, this must shatter the traditional view that training for diplomatic activity (to which we come back once more infra sub c and d) can or must lead to a comprehensive

[58] Report cited *supra* n. 55 at 908.
[59] The fact-gathering function is admirably discussed by Roger Hilsman, *strategic Intelligence and National Decisons,* Glencoe, Free Press (1956), after having once more evoked the historical image quoted.

idea of International Relations, that the 'field of Theory' is confined to the scientific basis needed by future diplomats or to the scientific analysis of what has been done by diplomats so far.

This view can only be described as a 'diplomato-morphic' view of International Relations, over-estimating the part of representatives in the forces that were at work, under-estimating the possibillity of analyzing those forces through *other* eyes than those of diplomats and their staff.

It is submitted that International Relations theory must beware of the 'over-political' emphasis and of its sub-division, the 'over-diplomatic' emphasis. Also of the tacit assumption that some 'human activity' can be *distilled* and put under a magnifying glass so as to give us the real 'nucleus' of the International Relations field. For that reason the word 'diplomato-morphic' view was purposely chosen: this view is like the 'anthropo-morphic' view we very frequently have of cosmic problems. It is sobering to see international life as a cosmic-historical phenomenon where human insight and endeavour, including the activity of rulers and diplomats, governments, politicians and learned or fanatic writers do but little change a slow course of events which we are not able to see as a whole, or which we look at with pre-Copernican bias and primitive instruments. Yet the modesty and resignation thus gained could erroneously be held to lead to moral despair: as long as we admit that human activity and, what is not the same, human insight can make some difference, however small, for better or worse, the moral task is not less than if we would boast that such activity and insight are indeed all there is to International Relations.

c. Diplomacy and the Actors on the Scene. When we consider the place of diplomacy as the 'representation of actors' in international politics we do well to remember the difference between 'states-as-the-sole-actors,' model of International Relations or as it has been aptly called by Arnold Wolfers,[60] 'the billiard-ball' model of the multi-state system and the 'deviations' of this model on account either of the

[60] Arnold Wolfers, 'The Actors in International Politics' in W.F.R. Fox ed.) *op. cit., supra* n. 6, at 83-106.
[61] *Id.* 101.

role of 'non-state corporate actors'[61] or of individuals in the international constellation. We must also keep in mind that diplomacy, taken as representation of the 'home-land' (or 'home-corporation' as the case may be) vis-a-vis foreign lands, is to a great extent, as I would call it, 'home-bound,' that is subject to the representative autority of the diplomat's home. Even the 'billiard-ball' model tells us little about the inner structures and 'dynamics' of the control of foreign relations. A major survey of the methods and machinery from the 'home' point of view has seldom been attempted, although one such recent attempt indeed provides both material and reflective theory on a very high level[62] and although, of course, the 'treaty making power' of states has been amply analysed. Representation in this sense is considered theoretically (and in habitual practice) so highly important, because it may further good relations or sweeten somewhat sour relations. It will be, so it is believed, the necessary springboard for diplomacy in the sense of negotiating, of enabling a nation to exert its full weight or of 'juggling for a favourable position.'

In this respect 'Diplomatic Practice' is really bewitching theory. Rules, fashions and usages have at one time given 'style' to diplomatic representative usage or 'protocol' and nowhere is 'legality' and 'behaviour' in international relations better integrated than in this respect. Immunities, precedence, formalities of some sort are 'conditio sine qua non' of both representation and negotiation between nations; many rules of International Law are quite often broken but the etiquette and protocol of diplomatic behaviour are more rigidly respected. It has therefore been suggested — erroneously it is submitted — that diplomacy could render services when International Law is breaking down. We will discuss this suggestion, particularly as presented by Prof. Morgenthau[63] (see infra sub d) but it must be admit-

---

[62] Philip W. Buck and Martin B. Travis Jr. (eds.), *Control of Foreign Relations in Modern Nations*, New York, W. W. Norton & Co. (1959).
[63] Hans J. Morgenthau in *Politics among Nations*, New York, Alfred A. Knopf (1948) 445. The present writer's criticism in Ch. Boasson, *Sociological Aspects of Law and International Adjustment*, Amsterdam, North Holland Publishing Co. (1950) 70, 75, 76. Against the over-political approach in general very convincingly, Wilhelm Wengler, *Der Begriff des Politischen im Internationalen Recht*, Tübingen, J. C. B. Mohr (1956) 30ff.

ted that to some extent diplomacy seems often still flourishing where International Law is withering away. The bedevilling aspect of such diplomatic activity as is constantly going on is that each diplomat seems caught in a treadmill of accepted activities such as scanning his post and newspapers, meeting worthies of his own state and the state to which he is accredited, visiting and being visited by his colleagues or the representatives of the host-state, attending official functions of a supposedly cultural, military or purely social character; and yet in the unavoidable treadmill, a 'bon-mot,' an earnest speech, an expression of joy or regret, a sincere wish or convincing act of solidarity after a calamity of some sort, a timely intervention or a wise restraint, may palpably improve conditions or avoid catastrophes. And of course the opposite is true: a clumsy remark, *a faux pas* or some stupidity may have disastrous consequences. It does not seem that these matters are so entirely different from any other human activity, but a nimbus of extraordinary responsibility has, naturally, grown round the diplomatic profession and together with it a theoretical assumption that 'good diplomacy' of some kind, whether that of summit conferences, or old-style secret negotiations[64] can save humanity. How far must we endorse this assumption?

The very opposite model, that of diplomats as powerless, somewhat senile, puppets dancing a grim dance of death, will not easily be found in serious theory. It has been presented however, to the world audience of art with shattering impact by the Kurt Jooss Ballet in 'The Green Table' for more than twenty five years. Its very impact has not been due only to the excellent dancing performance, but to the shock of recognizing the terrible meaning of such a model. As a model it is one-sided to the extreme, but we need not consider it a mere caricature. For even if diplomats are honest and capable, sincerely endeavouring to alleviate misery and to promote peace and understanding (as is, in fact, so often the case) they are severly limited both by forces outside their control and perhaps somewhat by the treadmill itself (ostentatious receptions, formal functions) without

---

[64] How many negotiations, by the way, are not better carried on behind closed doors? See the critical examination of arguments in favour of Summit Conferences in O. Harries 'Faith in the Summit: Some British Attitudes' *Foreign Affairs* (October 1961).

which they cease to remain diplomats, but because of which strivings for radical improvement may easily get blocked. More realistic than either of these extreme views, I submit, is one which sees diplomacy as an activity not altogether irrelevant to the constellation in which it eases mutual contact, but which is not an art able to change that constellation substantially merely by superior skill.

d Diplomacy and Political Behaviour. Most theories indeed agree that Diplomacy does influence the international constellation to a lesser or greater degree and admit that perhaps in extreme constellations there may be no scope left for Diplomacy. Obviously the aspect of Diplomacy stressed in such expositions is not the 'representative' but the 'accommodating,' in other words: the most effective accomodation of state relations that are sometimes in harmony but other times in conflict.[65] What is rather odd is that this flexible and uncommitted view of diplomacy very often seems to give rise to unbridled expectations of 'good diplomacy.' A book appeared recently under the title 'The Power of Small States, Diplomacy in World War II,' which says on its second page: 'For the Small State diplomacy is the tool of statecraft in whose use it can on occasion hope to excel. The representatives of great powers have more than once been outmatched at the conference table by the diplomats from the small states.'[66] Obviously this assumes a theoretical model where *survival* of these states depends to a great extent on their diplomatic ability. Yet this book, which is most objectively and informatively written throughout, admits at the outset that diplomatic excellence 'is often tied in with other means of getting support'[67] and concludes that 'not all the states studied had equal opportunities for diplomatic maneuver.'[68] Readers of this particular book, who might originally have shared this 'Survival-thanks-to-Diplomacy' assumption, may well close it with their

---

[65] Quotation from: Kenneth W. Thompson, *Political Realism and the Crisis of World Politics*, Princeton U.P. (1960) 224.
[66] Annette Baker Fox, *The Power of Small States*, University of Chicago Press (1959).
[67] *Id.* 2.
[68] *Id.* 180.

faith in this assumption shaken, having found in these excellent case Studies material 'for a different kind of analysis.'[69]

Among the extreme believers in 'Survival-thanks-to-Diplomacy' we find, naturally enough, I think, the so-called 'realists,' and a prominent example of these in our days is Hans J. Morgenthau, who pins all hopes for human survival, or for establishing the preconditions for permanent peace on stretches of short-term-peace, on 'peace through accommodation'. Its instrument is diplomacy.[70]

It is submitted that these 'realist' assumptions are far too simplistic. International life is pictured by them as a ruthless struggle for power where the only rules of behaviour of a-little-more-than-a-second's duration are those of diplomatic etiquette, and where moreover the party who is unable to make the most efficient use of the little lee-way thus given to him not only ruins his own country but all humanity. No doubt the mood of serious students occasionally inclines them to such a picture, as a serious man may occasionally echo the lamentation of Job: 'Let the day perish wherein I was born.' But that is one gloomy picture which we must place amongst many more pictures (some of them perhaps equally gloomy!) before it enlightens us in the slightest about what really happens in life. It seems so simple and 'true', but there are many situations where there is either no struggle for power, or where power is sought for not-easily-defineable interests, where the interest is not 'power', where the attempts to realize the interest can not even be squared with the supposedly overriding interest to amass power for 'survival.' The advice given by realists to diplomats is: 'to determine objectives in the light of the power actually and potentially available for the pursuit of these objectives.'[71] Admittedly in giving such advice to 'diplomats,' the intention is to include in this category rather the politicians who guide diplomatic ac-

[69] *Id.* VIII.

[70] Hans H. Morgenthau, (1948) *Politics Among Nations*, New York, Alfred A. Knopf 419. In the latest edition (the third, published in 1960) Morgenthau has kept his chapters on 'Diplomacy' and 'The Future of Diplomacy' virtually intact, increasing, if anything, his emphasis on the importance of diplomacy. See also his contribution on 'The Permanent Values in the Old Diplomacy,' Ch. 2 in Stephen D. Kertesz and M. A. Fitz Simmons (eds.), *Diplomacy in a Changing World*, Notre Dame U.P. (1959).

[71] Morgenthau, *ibid.*

tivities or take upon themselves the role of diplomatic representative. But the advice seems nevertheless of exaggerated simplicity.

The simplicity miscarries because it neglects the whole scale of adjustments; the *ranking order* in objectives; the *change* in objectives through factors, unconnected with diplomacy (or law, or wars); the change *unregistered* by diplomacy. It misses, in short, the point that diplomacy, even when extended to include diplomatic policy, is an art developed out of needs in world affairs but not possibly an art to satisfy *all* the needs in world affairs.

e. Diplomacy and the Political Constellation. According to our submission we obtained for 'Diplomacy' a model which we will meet again and again: the task, functions and methods of Diplomacy are to a great extent *given by ever changing constellations in* International Relations (and to this extent the Science and Art of Diplomacy are totally inadequate to give us a Theory of International Relations), but to some extent diplomatic activity, or perhaps diplomatic in-activity *does change the constellations.* To fathom both the extent to which it can do so, and the ways and means by which it may do so, is the proper field for theoretical analysis.[72] This means that the selection and education of diplomatic experts, including their 'picture' or mental model of diplomacy becomes the concern of theorists. Indeed we see that theory also influences the education of diplomats as well as the assignments given (or not given) to them. The analysis of conference diplomacy, or summit diplomacy and of the nostalgic longing for the classical diplomacy all properly form part of this theoretical concern. One assumption needs further attention, namely the assumption that in modern diplomacy there is no longer a 'community of language.' This brakdown of a common language is usually demonstrated by two somewhat opposite methods of proof: In the first place it is said that modern means of communication force the diplomat, or statesman, to act primarily for his 'home-market' and not for the purpose of accommodation. On this basis modern diplomats, and in particular those from Communist countries, are often accused of

[72] It is difficult to imagine a better or more sensitive appreciation of the diplomat's role than Sir William Hayter, *The Diplomacy of the Great Powers*, London, Hamish Hamilton (1961).

'*woodenness*', of inflexibility and an inability or unwillingness to seek accommodation.[73] It is submitted that such 'woodenness' may also have been present very often behind the velvet manners of classical diplomacy and that while the accusation may often enough be justified as far as the contemporary scene is concerned, without further refinement or an altogether different analysis we cannot say that a return to the 'old' diplomacy is all that is needed to save the world.

In the second place it is sometimes assumed that diplomatic deadlock results from a lack of common language, in the litteral sense of a world language. It is submitted that we have here a double misconception of the function of language: uniformity of language is not a requirement for proper understanding and lack of it therefore *in itself* no barrier, but the learning of a second or more languages opens up new possibilities of understanding humanity in general and is therefore a useful asset to the student of International Relations. It is submitted that a world-language, apart from such intrinsic, or nonpolitical attractions as it may have, is not in the slightest a stepping stone to world understanding and in some cases a common or a developed language serves as 'an adequate linguistic equipment — for quarreling.'[74] On the other hand it is stressed that the learning of a foreign language, whilst perhaps not necessary for learning International Relations Theory or entering the Diplomatic Service when the student has been educated in one of the 'major' languages, is a cultural enrichment without which, as a basis, the later scholar or diplomat may be seen as a 'crippled' person.

Most discussions of this problem, even in mono-linguistically educated countries, admit this, although against a background which sounds fantastic to the multi-linguistically educated. Even the latter seem not to be aware that by far the best age for basic language-

[73] An example is Philip E. Mosely, 'Some Soviet Techniques of Negotiations,' first published in Raymond Dennett and Joseph E. Johnson (eds.), *Negotiating with the Russians*, Boston (1951) republished by Alexander Dallin, *Soviet Conduct in World Affairs*, Columbia University Press (1960) 198-205.

[74] James H. S. Bossard, *The Sociology of Child Development*, New York, Harper & Bros. (1948) 235. I have developed the problem of language in international relations more fully in Chapter 3 ('Law and Verbal Expression') of *Sociological Aspects of Law and International Adjustment*, Amsterdam, North Holland Publishing Company (1950).

learning is not later than 8-14 and if elementary schools have missed this chance, patching up by secondary schools, colleges and universities remains defective. Reliable statements have been made that in 1958 only 50% of the U.S. Foreign Service Corps had a speaking knowledge of any foreign language; amongst the newly appointed this percentage was not more than 30%.[75] It is submitted that teaching of 'foreign' languages is not part of the teaching of International Relations theory proper, but that a working knowledge of one or two such language education is exceptional shows some basic defect in the educational system of most countries.

3. Geography

a. Geography and the Political Constellation. Geography, which in its primitive form is sometimes merely extended story-telling by travellers,[76] necessarily leads in the end to concepts which influence our thinking on International Relations.

If any specific country means more to a person than an absolute 'blank,' its name alone evokes an impressionistic picture of its natural setting and of its population in a social context. For instance during the centuries when the people of Israel were separated from their homeland such a picture persisted not only in the minds of the dispersed people but also, to some extent, in the minds of the other peoples amongst whom they dwelled.

The need[77] to keep the geographical picture — landscape, distance, climate and people — always in mind in thinking of international problems requires little elaboration; the more remarkable therefore is the enormous neglect of the environmental factors particularly in political treatises. This neglect may be partly ascribed to a desire to dis-

---

[75] From Richard N. Swift, *World Affairs and the College,* Washington D.C., Am. Council of Education (1959), 47. See further a sensible discussion by C. Dale Fuller, *Training of Specialists in International Relations,* Washington, D. C. American Council of Education (1957).

[76] See Marco Polo's fascinating *La Description du Monde,* (ed. Louis Hambia) Paris, C. Klincksieck (1955).

[77] See J. P. Cole, *Geography of World Affairs,* Harmondsworth, Penguin Special (1950).

count previous overemphasis on distances (measured in out-of-date units) as well as on so called 'natural' barriers (sometimes out-dated by technical changes); partly, it may have resulted from a — justifiable — reaction against the tainted ideology of 'geopolitics.' Yet it is incredible that Harold and Margaret Sprout had to be somewhat apologetical when they put the 'man-miliey'-relationship again in proper theoretical perspective.[78]

Those two authors give us the most satisfactory broad framework, leaving adequate room for social and other factors, not only from the viewpoint of basic geographical theory, where these social and similar factors must be placed in the total piture, but also from the political point of view where geographic *opinion* (whether correctly or *erroneously*[79] held) does influence decisions, and where geographic *conditions* influence again the results of the decisions when put into action. What these authors impress upon us irrefutably, I think, is the fact that even when political decisions are in part influenced by geographical assessment, the decision is not *a priori* calculable in terms of the basic geographic conditions, because the interdependence of environment and decision is ever developing, ever changing and needs constant reassessment. The frame-work is no doubt available, but the solution must always be found a new, in a chain of gradually (sometimes even abruptly) changing *historical* situations.

This is a problem which geographers in the 20th century[80] are struggling to delineate as much as former geographers were and future geographers will be struggling to do. There is no absolute freedom from climate[81], not even with oilomatic heaters, or with refriger-

[78] Harold and Margaret Sprout, *'Man-Milieu' Relationship Hypotheses in the Context of International Politics*, Princeton, Center of International Studies (1956); 'Environmental Factors in the Study of International Politics' (1957) *Jo. of Conflict Resolution* 309-328.

[79] This reference to possible error in opinion is an important remark made by the authors in their contribution on the 'New Ecology of International Politics' (1960) 4 *Journal of Conflict Resolution,* 148, and it could be adapted to viewpoints of *all* kinds in the theory of international relations.

[80] Griffith Taylor (ed.), *Geography in the 20th Century*, London, Methuen (1951), 3rd ed. (1957).

[81] Stephen Sargent Visher, 'Climate Influences' in Taylor, *id.* Chapter x 196-220.
S. F. Markham, *Climate and the Energy of Nations,* New York, Oxford University

ation and air-conditioning, but there is also no 'determination' which is not capable of being *unexpectedly* broken by new inventions. These make stop-and-go determinism very flexible indeed. They upset estimates of 'Possibilism' and even 'Probabilism' as Harold and Margaret Sprout were able to demonstrate in respect of Cressey's fantastic underestimation of Russia's technological progress, only six years after Cressey's publication.[82] Not only is calculation often proved wrong soon after it has been earnestly, perhaps competently, attempted, but even instructions on how to calculate, or how to estimate proportional importance, may soon be outdated in the same way.

Anyone dealing open-mindedly with the interaction between nature and society will soon reconsider his own apodictic statements. The present writer stated recently:[83] '. . .civilization then is partly a creation of . . . and partly, but essentially, re-creating the crude geographic and climate situation. Historians and lawyers alike are apt to overrate the geographic setting as the more solid or nearly immutable factor and consesequently to consider human relations as greatly moulded in submission and as adaptation to this fixed framework of nature.'

Yet, there may, in a different constellation, be historians and lawyers engaged in the most gross under-estimation of the frame-work of nature, which not always yields to legal decisions; or which, under ever spreading over-consumption or neglect, may refuse to yield the desired product at all.

The geographical point of view makes us very much aware of the interdependence of a great many factors of which, in conclusion, we cannot say more than that International Relations theory must take them into account, although the exact accounts of the interrelationships are forever fluid, unfinished.

Press (1944) (revised after an English edition of 1942). Also, of course, the work of Ellsworth Huntington, *Principles of Economic Geography*, New York, John Wiley & Sons (1940), *passim*.

[82] G. B. Cressey, *How Strong is Russia?*, Syracuse University Press (1954). See *Journal of Conflict Resolution*, Vol. IV (1961) 157.

[83] Ch. Boasson, 'Sociological Excursions along International Rivers' in *Symbolae Verzyl*, The Hague, Martinus Nijhoff (1958) 53.

b. Geography and Political Growth. It is submitted that most of the theoretical problems which emerge in considering International Relations from the geographical point of view give a clear indication of the fundamental problems which any other approach, when diligently pursued, will also reveal. Some of these problems — which will always recur therefore in International Relations theory — may be summarized as follows:

Firstly: technical development upsets many historical assumptions (barriers are no longer obstacles, resources can be tapped in different ways, adverse climate can be easier to bear etc.) but not all historical assumptions lose importance.

Secondly: Technical development requires social preparedness, a minimal educational level, before it can be usefully applied to more than a wealthy fringe of the population.[84]

Thirdly: Social preparedness goes hand in hand with political maturity, which is partly education and partly sheer tradition, a slowly *grown* (not merely taught) mutual tolerance. Of course the habit of good neighbourliness (which also presupposes reciprocity) normally transcends local frontiers.

Fourthly: Geographic regions therefore are determined as much by accidental natural constellations (rivers, climate, resources) as by historical, social and political processes. One cannot at will transplant methods of government, economy, industry and transport without adaptation.

Fifthly: There exist favourable conditions (modereate climate, fertile soil, accessability of resources, facilities for transport and trade, possibilities of cultural exchange and enrichment) which, when exploited (which is not always the case of course) give the favoured regions or populations an advantage which technical development is not likely to equalize *but rather to accentuate:* 'intercourse between the more developed and less developed areas, while contributing to rising levels of living on both sides, appears to have produced greater increases in the more developed than in the less. To attribute this result to colonial rule is much too simple . . . most of the less developed

[84] Daniel Lerner *et al, The Passing of Traditional Society,* Glencoe, Free Press (1958).

countries which escaped colonial rule have been equally slow, or even slower in economic growth.'[85]

Sixthly: The exploitation of favourable conditions often leads to a scandalous waste[86] which frustrates the best human efforts to control or eliminate it.[87]

Seventhly: Techniques of trade and of war can overcome frontiers and barriers which once upon a time seemed absolute. 'The man-milieu combination has made shambles of those natural barriers. . . the weaponry of defense has lagged behind the weaponry of attack. . . strategies of defense have corrupted into strategies of reprisal.'[88] Theoretically each state can chose its own trading partner as well as its own enemy, reachable by fast plane or ballistic missile. In fact the geography of *contiguity*, whether of trade, culture-constract or conflict, is not altogether superseded.

Eigthly: The geographic point of view is far from monolithic:[89] it depends on climatology and adequate meteorology, soil-science, biology, human-factor analysis, economies, technology[90] with great emphasis on the development of transport, political and social science.

c. Geography and Human Endeavour. There is a tendency in geographical literature to develop theory from the given setting of natural conditions to human and social interference, which change those conditions. This easily leads geographers to rate industrial and urban society as 'developed' — in a positive sense — and to estimate the more primitive society as, in a negative sense, *under*-developed. No

---

[85] Cf. Richard Hartshorne, 'Geography and Economic Growth' in *Essays on Geography and Economic Development,* Norton Ginsburg (ed.), University of Chicage Press (1960) 14.

[86] Ch. Boasson, *op. cit., supra* n. 83, 60.
Richard L. Meyer, *Science and Economic Development* asks: 'How much production is enough?' New York, Technology Press and John Wiley (1956) 237.

[87] Hartshorne, *id.* 6, 3.

[88] J. David Singer, 'The Geography of Conflict: Introduction' (1961) IV *Jo. of Conflict Resolution 3.*

[89] Systematic treatment, with suggestive diagrams, in Griffith Taylor, *op. cit. supra.* n. 80, 45 ff.

[90] Willian Fielding Ogburn (ed.). *Technology and International Relations,* University of Chicago Press (1949).

one has adequately defined 'over-developed' or 'de'-naturalized, except perhaps a few 'naturalist' idealizers and dreamers or critics of 'waste-making'[91] or of the 'affluent society'.[92] It is submitted that even here we need 'relevant' utopias.[93]

It seems that much more 'development' goes into conflict patterns ('defense', as quoted before 'deteriorated into reprisals') than into cooperative patterns, or cultural efforts.

It is obvious that strategic development leads to strategic vulnerability: at the same time, awareness of this leads more or less automatically to an expectation that vulnerability invites attack, and that therefore there is a need for the building up of aggressive deterrents.

d. Geography and Population Trends. The expectations suggested by development-considerations will be re-inforced by the normal demographic considerations. Now it must not be assumed that demography which must focus its attention on population-factors in preference to environmental factors, thereby belittles the importance of those very environmental factors. Sound demography consists not in a rejection of some geographical hypotheses, but in directing the magnifying glass on all the aspects of population-growth and population-'quality,' such as health, education[94] and the division of labour. This necessarily leaves the problem of man-milieu relationship intact. In so far as demography analyzes the educational levels, the 'dark areas of ignorance' in respect of international affairs, the patterns which make for aggressiveness,[95] this is a rather late development and in any case

---

[91] Vance Packard, *The Waste makers*, London, Longmans (1960).
[92] J. K. Galbraith, *The affluent Society*, London, Hamish Hamilton (1958).
[93] Richard L. Meyer, 'Science and Economic Development' in *New Patterns of Living*, Massachusetts Institute of Technology (1956) 218.
[94] Cf. Dael Wolfle (ed.), *America's Resources of Specialized Talent*, New York, Harper & Bros. (1954).
[95] In anticipation of our later analysis two pioneer studies must be mentioned in advance, and their title is indicative of their importance: Harold D. Lasswell, *World Politics and Personal Insecurity* (1935!) (Reprinted in *A Study of Power*, Glencoe, Free Press, (1950). Talcott Parsons, Certain Primary Sources and Patterns of Aggression in the Social Structure of the Western World' (1947), *Psychiatry* 10: 167 ff. (repr. *Essays in Sociological Theory*, Glencoe, Free Press, (rev. ed. 1954).

is most intimately interwoven with developments in political and social science (see infra Ch. IV).

The classical demographic statement of a, (if not *the*), problem of International Relations is of course the Malthusian image of 'population pressure.'

Two submissions are hereby made in connection with the Malthusian aspect of International Relations:

a. in the first place the problem is not one limited to demographic trends, division of expanding, shrinking or moving populations. Even the moving of populations from rural to urban areas is interlocked with emotional problems of living, of security, of education and the problem therefore branches out into many sub-problems, mainly of a sociological character[96]. Problems of economics, of war and peace, of such a vague but important concept as 'happiness' are related to, but not determined by 'absolute numbers', even if such a dictum is 'speculative.'[97] One of the most fertile suggestions in this respect is that of Gaston Bouthoul[98] building on similar suggestions by Corrado Gini,[99] who stressed the importance of the age-group of late adolescents and young adults in the total demographic picture.

b. in the second place there seems to be a practically universal dishonesty and harmful false-shame in respect of the problem of conscious and technical (that is other than by the Ogino-Knauss, or 'calendar' method) birth-control.[100] This is related probably to the refusal to acknowledge that much religious fanaticism has chosen the side of the persecutors, hunters for obscenity, despisers of either or both of the sexes and above all haters of sexual harmony and of the idea of sexual attraction not exclusively in the service of procreation (whether

---

[96] It is interesting that such a serious excellent book as J. O. Hertzler, *The Crisis in World Population*, University of Nebraska Press (1956), does not mention the suggestions of Bouthoul referred to hereafter. It shows much there is to be worked on the population aspect.

[97] Ch. Boasson in *Research for Peace, op. cit. supra* n. 12, 208, 211.

[98] Gaston Bouthoul, *Les Guerres*, Paris, Payot (1951).

[99] C. Gini, *I fattori demografici*, quoted by Bouthoul, *ibid.*
C. Gini (ed.), *Population*, Chicago (1930) quoted by Quincy Wright, *A Study of War*, Vol. II., esp. Chapter XXXI, Univ. of Chicago Press (1942).

[100] W. F. Cottrell, in *Research for Peace, op. cit. supr* n. 12 152ff.
Ch. Boasson, *id.* 210ff.

the off-spring be wished for or not). Many authors have tried to by-pass this aspect of international relations theory altogether, or, even worse, have referred to it by innuendo, fearful of becoming conscious of the fact, 'that, if need be, the growth in population can be checked by other means than the traditional ones' (sic!).[101] It is a hopeful sign that in literary circles this play at hide-and-seek is being more and more exposed. Scientific enquiry might with profit follow suit.[102]

4. History

a. History and Awareness. From whatever angle we have looked at International Relations we have not been able to avoid using histori-cal and developmental categories.

Vice versa, there can be now no alert historian at work, who is not concerned in his whole being with contemporary problems, and also with future problems or expectations — whether fearful or optimistic — about those future problems. These expectations can colour the conceptions and constructions of the historian to a dangerous extent. Those who had their secondary-school or university education after, say, 1920 and not much later than 1935 might (some indeed did) re-ceive history-lessons pointing to the development from small primi-tive warring communities to ever growing regions of peaceful order, crowned by the final superb edifice of the League of Nations. Since the crash of this edifice there have not been as many teachers, certain-ly not at the University level, with a like simplicity of belief in the new edifice,[103] or in the possibility of some other better one to grow out of it. Has the pendulum swung back too far?

[101] Trygve Mathisen, *Methodology in the Study of International Relations*, Oslo Univ. Press (1959).

[102] This combination of love-of-war, intolerant government prying into literature and art, witch-burning and xenophobia is competently exposed by a Dutch literary critic, Jacques Den Haan, in the monthly *Maastaf* of 1961, referring a.o. to Ken-neth Allsop and Robert Ditman, *A Question of Obscenity*, Northwood, Scorpion Press (1960).

Holbrook Jackson, *The Fear of Books*, London, Soncino Press (1932). Most enligh-tening is also *The Trial of Lady Chatterley,* Harmondsworth, Penguin Special (1961).

[103] A notable exception, a naive example (more representative of a school-teacher's

Do some historians, over-concerned to find unbiassed truth and respecting documentation more than vision, tell their story as a 'tale full of sound and fury, signifying nothing?' This question concerns us in two ways. Since in the first place it is true as Raymond Aron asserts, that only the historical-sociological approach to any situation of conflict[104] (or, I would say, to any international situation whatsoever) can give us a full idea of what we are talking about, we must delve deeper into the meaning and portent of historical contemplation. Secondly, we are concerned because the study of history, historical consciousness, may or may not lead to the study and consciousness of International Relations. In order to see in how far this historical concern (not *for* but with International Relations) is a 'conditio sine qua non' for historians in general and not only for specialists amongst the historians, we can not avoid entering into a discussion, apparently an eternal one, of what historians are telling us.

b. History and Personalities or Trends. The discussion will not be about whether any historian tries to tell us a story 'signifying nothing' *to him*. No one is doing that. It will be concerned with whether, in terms of the questions asked (by implication perhaps) and the moods expressed, the story means much to anyone else. The learned professor, asked to lecture on some general aspects of the 16th century, who replied indignantly that 'his whole life task was his national history between 1525-1530,' meant, perhaps, that not only his own competence did not go beyond these limits but that no one's historical general opinion should be taken seriously. Yet obviously what is most serious to one historian, or to one period, does not seem so to others or to another period. It depends (See supra CH. II, 4) on prevalent opinions and moods.

---

attitude than of a University textbook) of unsurpassed belief in perhaps 'automatic' progress is Gerard J. Mangone, *A Short History of International Organizations,* New York, McGraw Hill (1954). From the Preface (p.v.) 'Important as the UN. may be, for example, it is here regarded as a part of a more vital process which has been going on for centuries'.

[104] Raymond Aron, 'Conflict and War from the Viewpoint of Historical Sociology' in *The Nature of Conflict* (eds. Jessie Bernard, T. H. Pear, Raymond Aron, Robert C. Angell), Paris, UNESCO (1957), Cf. supra, this ch. sub. 1.

If former historians have stressed the heroic stature of personalities, later emphasis has shifted — following to no mean extent the lead of Leo Tolstoy in his 'War and Peace' — toward the social aspect of any 'story.' By 1931, Leonard Woolf, a profound thinker on the essence of history and a fascinating story teller, would call (in a derogatory sense) those, who see history 'as a necklace of great men and famous or infamous names,': 'biographers and psychologists rather than historians.'[105]

We need not discuss at length how each historian 'has to consider the scale of time against which he is to measure and judge events,'[106] how 'historical thinking is always directed towards some finality or goal. The past supplies the material; the glance is cast in retrospect, the mind is aware that not a minute of the future can be really predicted, yet it is the eternal future which moves this very mind.'[107]

However, we must ask ourselves whether historians, by writing against scales of time, against scales of a complex incalculable interplay of forces, can evolve a relevant International Relations 'sense'. Historians are, of course, not responsible for facile ideas about an automatic evolution towards 'International Society,' 'World Government,' 'Federalism,' 'Peaceful Balance of Powers,' 'Collective Security' and so on. Nor are they responsible for unhistorical slogans like 'Recurrent Warfare,' 'l'Histoire se repète', and similar catchwords.

Historians, however, must supply us with a sufficient awareness of the relative 'undeterminedness' of a course of events which is not entirely undetermined, which can not be altered beyond the boundaries set by some prerestined limitations. Human effort, constructive as well as destructive, tendencies and their counterpart can be placed by historians, tentatively, in retrospect. Are these historical reflections helpful for International Relations Theory?

---

[105] Leonard Woolf, *After the Deluge*, London, The Hogarth Press, (1931), Pelican Ed., Harmondsworth (1937) 47.
[106] Leonard Woolf, *id.* 57.
[107] J. Huizinga, *De Wetenschap der Geschiedenis*, originally published in Spanish 'Sobre el Estado Actual de la Ciencia Historia,' Madrid, *Revista de Occidente* (1934), later in Dutch (1934-35; also 1937) and finally in the Collected Works *Verzamelde werken*, vol. 7, Haarlem, H. D. Tjeenk Willink (1950) 104ff. at 138.

c. History and Wisdom. It is difficult enough for historians to render account of the growth of a city, a group or a nation without even having to consider the international framework of the past. Some historians have no doubt been critical of their own group or nation; they may have criticized even a *way* of living, but they could not well have doubted the *right* to live or to exist of the group they were describing, if it happened to be their own group.

History is partly the *justification* of — the seeking of an *excuse* for — what we are.

The historian who searches for radical alternatives to what has come into existence ceases to be a historian! There are many such 'ex-historians' and we should be careful even about the utopian standards which they purport to distil from the lessons of history. Nor should we trust their historical exposition completely, at least not without detached criticism. The historian's bias in interpreting the past is perhaps the minor problem (to which I will revert in Ch. IV once more). The more important one is his lack of standards for dealing with *unprecedented* problems, the fact that his wisdom is drawn from and can only be drawn from what *has been* under the sun. This clash of possibility with impossibility, vitiates so much of the historian's spade-work for international theory. Therefore it frequently really happens that, as Anatole France has suspected and described with his — not always — benevolent humour, historians are either excusing their own interest or are *frivolous!*[108]

There need be no frivolity in studying histories of former wars, of federations, of governments, of political 'adventures' when these are measured against the scale of our own future. Frivolity enters when the past and the future are lightheartedly equated and if repeatperformances are easily assumed to be feasible. Yet lessons can not very well be learned from the unknown future and may be learned, *to some extent*, from the past. There have been gigantic attempts to de-

---

[108] '*Sans doute les raisons scientifiques de préférer un témoignage à un autre sont parfois très fortes. Elles ne le sont jamais assez pur l'emporter sur nos passions, nos préjugés, nos intérêts, ni pur vaincre cette légèreté d'esprit commune à tous les hommes graves. En sorte que nous présentons constamment les faits d'une manière intéressée ou frivole.*'
Preface, l'Ile des Pingouins.

fine this 'some extent' in an objective manner, but it is submitted that these attempts, in spite of their occasional immediate attractiveness and popularity are bound to deceive and ultimately disappoint their staunchest supporters. It can be admitted that these attempts start from the correct assumption that bias colours analysis. However, the degree of bias and the required dose of corrective compensation usually escape adequate measurement.

Major social and intellectual movements have shown an exaggerated belief in their own objectivity when suggesting a corrective for pre-existing social bias. Marxism has demonstrated, irrefutably, the existence of class prejudices; its remedy however, has been far from an objectively deduced criterion, and has been inspired by utopian, revolutionary models.[109]

There are other examples of allegedly objective attempts to analyze historical periods and cultural trends. It is submitted that none of these examples — which can be chosen more or less at random — do more than indicate vague re-assessments of 'utopian' or 'idealistic' pre-judgements, without succeeding in establishing objective standards, or 'spheres of the truth as such.'[10]

It may perhaps be said that the more radical the attempt to find an ever-valid corrective to bridge the gap between objective historical contemplation and 'utopian' or 'ideal' model, the more confused or fantastic the result becomes. In our own theory on theory this is not really astonishing, because 'objectivity' would require a simultaneousness of various — probably contradictory — ideal types which would immediately cause it to become too vague and meaningless. It would seem that the moderation and reasonableness of a point of view is much more important general acceptability. The most ambitious sample of an attempt to objectify history is of course the so-called 'Sociology of Knowledge,' which is not restricted to one author or one single solution. Yet the work of Mannheim may be taken as representing this approach, and *Ideology and Utopia* as typical of its inability to

---

[109] For an interesting discussion of the non-objective accidentals in Marxism see J. Barzun, *Darwin, Marx, Wagner*, Boston, Little Brown & Co. (1941) Anchor Book (1958) 169-196.
[110] See, for example, Karl Mannheim, *Ideology and Utopia*, New York (1936) first Harvest Book ed. Harcourt, Brace & Co. (no date, but not before 1953).

produce the one relevant 'truthful' utopia for all time and every situation. Another life-time's attempt at establishing three 'Super-Systems' of ethics, law and personality (or cultural-types) came from Pitirim A. Sorokin; yet his proposed curves, percentages and charts[111] seem playthings for anyone who is not standing on exactly the same vantage point as Sorokin.

Another attempt at establishing the utopian time-sense and future-expectation as an objective measurement is given in an extremely learned compilation by Fred L. Polak, 'De toekomst is verleden tijd' 1960, (The future is past time'), a book as fantastic as its claim of having introduced for the first time the conception of the future as a general catagory of scientific social thought. The weight of its quotations, however, leave us no objective standards, but re-state the truism that often the expectations of the future colour the deductions from the past.

d. History and Prediction. The problems raised by those seekers for an objective scale balancing between interpretation of the past and expectation of the future are of course of immense importance for the theory of International Relations. If it were true that such an objectifier could be construed, that falsifications in the interpretation of the past could be rectified or at least measured, we might be able to deduct from the past standards of planning for the future and politics, whether on a small or international scale, might become scientific. There is ample suggestion by Karl R. Popper[112] that scientific planning when on a small enough scale when freed from a fanatic belief in 'Inexorable Laws of Historical Destiny',[113] when limited to 'Piecemeal' as opposed to Utopian engineering,[114] can proceed on scientific lines even though the 'future' can not be foretold. Of all the attempts to analyze the past with a planning mind, perhaps for the purpose of

---

[111] Pitirim A. Sorokin, *Society Culture and Personality*, New York, Harper & Bros. (1947) Ch. 42, 620ff. Cf. my criticism in *Sociological Aspects of Law and International Adjustment*, Amsterdam, North Holland Publishing Cy. (1950).
[112] Karl R. Popper, *The Poverty of Historicism*, London, Routledge & Kegan Paul (1957).
[113] *Id.* 'Dedication,' p.v.
[114] *Id.* Ch. 21, 64ff.

planning, this is the most logical, careful and suggestive. It takes its 'ideal' of 'expected' type at a very, very short distance from the 'what we found or find in the historical or contemporary process'. Yet, paradoxically enough, the criticism levelled against Popper by a philosopher who adopts a Marxist creed, seems, it is submitted, basically correct and for our theoretical quest of the utmost importance. Alastair MacIntyre[115] has, also justly it is submitted, criticised 'the contemporary human sciences as nonhistorical, atomistic, content with limited, low-level generalisations, and unable to discern or construct theories of overall social structure.'[116] He then takes Prof. Popper to task for 'presenting us with pairs of what are alleged to be exclusive and exhaustive alternatives'[117] but these alternatives may be 'false' and MacIntyre objects to a dichotomy 'which allows us only to be *either* historicists *or* without any overall view of history.'[118] This is one aspect of a problem which, I believe, International Relations theory must face. It is connected with two other aspects of this problem: it may be that 'because *some* of the past is known, some of the future can be foretold . . . Thus one deals, not in certainties, but in probabilities.'[119] If this is so do we not need also, as well as listening to the past, to develop a deep anti-historical desire, a desire to improve matters? Or, to put it in the often misquoted but profound words of Nietzsche, is it not true that 'Man is something that should be overcome.'?[120] If this approach is adopted, history is for International Relations theory suggestive, but no more. What kind of suggestions are fruitful to a considerable degree still remains to be considered.[121] It is

[115] Alastair MacIntyre, 'Breaking the Chains of Reason' in E. P. Thompson (ed.) *Out of Apathy*, London, Stevens & Sons (1960), 195 ff.
[116] *Id*. 216.
[117] *Ibid*.
[118] *Id*. 217.
[119] This is a quotation (with italics added) from G. J. Renier, *History, Its Purpose and Method*, London, George Allen and Unwin (1950), where Renier discusses amply the theories of Anatole France 135-142.
[120] Compare Walter Kaufmann, *Nietzsche*, Princeton University Press (1950), Meridian ed. (1956) 268 and 127: 'The goal of humanity can not lie in the end (*Ende*) but only in its highest specimens.' Perhaps (adds Kaufmann) there is no more basic statement of Nietzsche's philosophy in all his writings than this sentence.
[121] See *supra*. This Chapter sub. 1.

further submitted, however, that this fusion of historical 'listening' and supra-historical planning or 'mending' can be found in such an eminent analyst of both historical and foreign-policy processes as Max Beloff when he writes, in compliance with definite instructions to indicate the historical foundations of the European Movement: 'It can therefore be said that the emergence of a strong movement for the reshaping of the European system on nem lines was not simply a product of international idealism foreschadowed in the previous century but represented, rather, the recognition of an undoubted fact, the collapse of the old European balance beyond repair.'[122] Now Beloff in writing this had, so to speak an implied 'commission'; namely to outline not only the need for a United Europe but also its historical unavoidability and few commissioned historians would have been so honest as to admit that the starting point for a new course in history is not more than plain recognition of the ruins of the past. To admit this is to admit how little guidance is given by historical lessons at critical moments.

5. Law

a. Law and the Origins of International Thinking. The legal approach to international relations has posited some of the most relevant utopian assumptions and yet, at the same time, has heavily overestimated the smooth realisability of its own-seemingly near but actually most distant — goals.

This neglect of the distance existing between the easily available and the dimly attainable has inevitably led to serious disillusion for most international lawyers. It is to some extent possible to indicate some of the necessarily basic assumptions of International Law together with the oft mistaken and misleading statements in the theory of international law to which these assumptions have given occasion.

If we take Ruyssen's interpretation of Francisco Vitoria,[123] who

---

[122] Max Beloff, *Europe and the Europeans*, London, Chatto & Windus (1957) 63.

[123] Theodore Ruyssen, *Les Sources doctrinales de l'internationalisme*, Paris, Presses Universitaires de France, 2 Vols. (1958). In Vol. 1 536, Vitoria is quoted as follows: '... *le droit n'a pas seulement la force d'une convention ou d'un pacte entre les hommes, mais bien celle d'une loi. Le monde entier qui, en quelque sorte, ne for-*

was one of the early founders of what is commonly called Modern International Law, we find a basic assumption which is the most inspring 'model' for any International Relations theory whatsoever. This model was akin to the prophetic vision of Isaiah in which 'nation shall not lift up sword against nation.' An interesting peculiarity of the Vitorian 'model' is that it seems untainted by the practically universal misconception of state-'independence' and instead is based on the notion of a 'political community' in which states are 'interdependent.'[124] Indeed two related and absurd doctrines in classical International Law were developed as deviations from the model of Vitoria and these deviations seem obstinately persisted in until our own days. State-sovereignty (or 'independence') is a negation of law and so is, in the last resort, even the minor evil, the doctrine that a state is never bound by laws or a legal system to which it has not expressly adhered, the so called doctrine of 'voluntarism.'

It is true indeed, that the conception of a 'Community of States' or a 'World Community' was, and probably still is *to some extent,* utopian. Yet it is the only basic model which can be conceived and at the same time, however vaguely, make sense for the useful study of International Relations and, a fortiori, for the useful assertion that there exists something like International Law.

b. Law: A World Community? If the ideal conception of a world-society or a word-community[125] is necessary because otherwise there exist neither law nor a relationship which makes the world as a whole meaningful, this does not mean that we can indicate precisely the qualities of such a community or the ways in which we can relevantly compare it to smaller communities. No doubt lawyers have been the first and the most daring in specifying the qualities, or at least the

---

me qu'une communauté politique, a le pouvoir de porter les lois justes ordonnées au bien de tous, qui constituent le droit de gens.'
[124] *Id.* 349ff. It cannot be said of course that in all respects Vitoria would now appear modern or liberal, but he was then a pioneer thinker from whom we can still learn.
[125] The Toenniesian distinction between a society and (a more intimately integrated) community is often of great importance in social science. However it is also often used where it can only bring confusion and in the present context it would do so.

legal attributes, of the international community and, it is submitted, in doing so they have often ruined the conception or made it misleading instead of helpful.

The trouble with the conceptions of International Law is not that they tend to be utopian; it may be said that every conception of law tends towards the utopian in that every such conception assumes a greater measure of justice and a greater extent of social integration or of popular acceptance of the Law than probably ever exist, even in the national sphere. The trouble with so many conceptions of International Law is that their utopian elements tend to lose relevance by following analogies of the national law systems whilst such analogies need thoughtful adaptation, not only or not principally on the level of law-technique,[126] but on the level of sociological analysis.[127] Some have denied the existence of an international community and most of those have perforce denied the legal character of International Law. Some have left it as a question: does an international community exist at all?[128] And such an outstanding jurist as De Visscher had defined the existence of an international community as 'one of the human mind — not corresponding to an effectively established order.' The main weakness, according to De Visscher, is the insufficient legal control of force.[129] Another Belgian theoretician J. Haesaert, for that reason thinks that there is no law-forming international community but a system of 'force' which subjects (in a figurative sense we might say which 'terrorizes') law altogether.[130] It is likely that even law in a well integrated community idealizes the degree of community-inte-

---

126 Compare H. Lauterpacht, *Private Law Sources and Analogies of International Law*, London, Longmans (1927).

127 Julius Stone, *Legal Controls of International Conflict*, London, Stevens & Sons (1954). Ch. Boasson, *Sociological Aspects of Law and International Adjustment*, Amsterdam, North Holland Publishing Cy. (1950).

128 Charles de Visscher, *Théories et Réaltés en Droit International Public,,:* Chapitre II 117-131 *'y a-t-il une communauté internationale?'* The answer: *'La communauté internationale est un ordre en puissance dans l'esprit des hommes; elle ne correspond pas à un ordre effectivement établi' (ibid).*

129 *Ibid.*

130 J. Haesaert, 'Les preténdus principes généraux de la politique internationale et du droit des gens. Académie Royale de Belgique. *Bulletin de la Classe des Lettres et des Sciences Morales et Politiques* (1950-57) 354-386, in particular 378.

gration ('we all behave like that,' 'this is our law and our sense of justice' — although not all the members of the community share the behaviour of the sense of justice). It is submitted that in many respects the international community is more than a mere ideal conception and is sufficiently integrated, though very imperfectly so to make the term 'International Law' permissible. International Relations theory must watch keenly what legal theory has to struggle with in this respect, and some recent careful rephrasing of old International Law slogans are worth analyzing, as we shall presently see. However, international lawyers themselves have an immense task before them, as was clearly stated half a century ago[131] and has been recently emphasized by Julius Stone, who has concentrated practically all the pertinent material, commented on this material in a series of enlightening and provocative 'discourses' and has re-formulated the as yet unfinished task thus: 'then international lawyers can no longer be content merely to affirm or deny the reality of international law or of the international community *en bloc*, but must accept Max Huber's challenge to assess, in the light of the facts, the *degree* and *precise location* of this reality, within the mass of traditional materials of international law.'[132]

c. Law and Integration of the Community. The most obvious model to imagine, when we find a community not well integrated, is the model of the *not yet fully* developed, or 'primitive' community and this is indeed, what we often find cited as the reason for the 'weakness' of international Law. It is submitted that this is fallacious and highly misleading. To follow a learned discussion on the tenets of International Law, any such discussion for the last few centuries, and then to call such law 'primitive' is patently absurd. The danger of the 'primitive community' model lies not merely in its cheap optimism ('everything will gradually grow in its right shape!'), but in its total

---

[131] Max Huber, *'Beitraege zur Kenntnis der sociologischen Grundlagen des Völkerrechts und der Staatengesellschaft'* (1910) 4. *Jahrbuch des öffentlichen Rechts der Gegenwart* 57ff. Reprinted (1928); also in collected essay (1948).
[132] Julius Stone, *op. cit. supra*, n. 127, Chs. II and IX, pp. 37ff., at 46 (italics in original).

misjudgment of the desintegrating forces at work[133] and its insufficient awareness of developmental chances (that is to say minimal
chances ocurring here and there only), towards fuller integration. The
jurist and the International Relations theorist in general must learn
from one another and must both admit the incompleteness and
vagueness of the model ('a community not strongly integrated').

d. Law and Membership of the Community, If, so some extent, there
exists an international community, it is not all clear who are the
members of this community. Perhaps this is already a mistaken question, for the question in this form makes tacit assumptions of this
kind: a community normally consists of individuals as members, the
laws of the community are binding on the individuals and if International Law is rather binding on states than on individuals, it is better
to say that states are members of the international community, even
though there are some sort of 'sub'-members such as organizations
and even though individuals can have advantages (or disadvantages)
thanks to their being part of a state or through the activity of an organization.

It is submitted that this is not a good model, not so much because
of the strictly legal reasoning involved, but because of its inadequacy
as a starting point for the understanding of the complicated, obtuse
ways in which the human, cultural, economic and social solidarity of
mankind works over frontiers and has repercussions in seemingly remote regions of the earth.[134] Even the more legal discussions of the
'membership' of the international community show interesting recent
developments which indicate the weakness of the model used, not
only formerly, but even now.

In former days membership in the international community could
be disrepectfully compared to a 'club'-membership. The echo's of this
club-mentality still resound in serious and (in other respects) up-to-
date textbooks. Such an eminent modernist as the late Hersh Lauterpacht left intact these 19th century sentences: 'The conception of International Persons is derived from the conception of the Law of Na-

[133] Ch. Boasson, *op. cit. supra* n. 127, at 10, n. 10.
[134] Cf. The 'Billiard-ball' model and its inadequacy in the diplomacy doctrine, *supra,* this Ch. Section 2.

tions. As this law is the body of rules which the civilized states consider legally binding in their intercourse, every state which belongs to the civilized states, and is therefore a member of the Family of Nations, is an International Person'.[135] Civilized meant for a long time, somewhat interchangeably, Christian, West-European or advanced in the techniques of warfare. The revolt against this club-membership-mentality is not new, was not alien to the approach of Lauterpacht himself, and has recently been forcefully formulated by Gesina Van der Molen, whose avowed Christian approach and whose belonging to a Calvinist university, makes her insistance on 'universality' even more meaningful.[136] Apart from that, her insistance on a 'universal law valid in all parts of the world' nevertheless takes adequate cognizance of regional groupings and regional developments influenced by regional legal philosophy. Heterogeneity in the membership of the international community and, at the same time, the greater 'uniqueness' of a composite member ('a State') than of individuals in each state, detracts from the universality of the Law of Nations,[137] but, as indicated before, the juridical construction of binding law through the intermediary of membership in the form of collectives, needs further elaboration. The more liberal admission of fullyfledged or half-willingly accepted members to the Club of 'civilized' nations is not enough.

e. Law and the Use of Force. A legal conception of the international community usually assumes — correctly — that the as yet imperfectly integrated community can be, and indeed must be, further consolidated and that, for that purpose, the use of force must be brought under control and the competence to decide conflicts given to an authoritative body, preferably judges (or arbitrators) but eventually a po-

[135] L. Oppenheim, *International Law* (8th ed. by H. Lauterpacht), London, Longmans Green & Co. (1955).
[136] Gesina H. J. van der Molen 'The Present Crisis in the Law of Nations' in *Symbolae Verzijl*, The Hague, Martinus Nijhoff, (1958) 238-254 at 250. See also B. V. A. Röling, *International Law in an Expanded World*, Amsterdam, Djambatan (1960) who gives a pointed discussion of the meaning of 'The Christian Nations,' 'The Civilized Nations' and 'The Peace Loving Nations,' Chapters III, IV and V.
[137] A problem discussed by J. L. Brierly *The Outlook for International Law*, London, Oxford Univ. Press (1944) 40ff.

litical body. Probably it is impossible to conceive the growth of law and the consolidation of any community otherwise than in such a way. The deceptiveness of this assumption, however, lies, it is submitted, in the tacitly assumed force of a legal pronunciamento. It is fair enough to direct this reproach less at serious international lawyers individually than at meetings of drafsmen at, or preparatory to peace-conferences. It is submitted that the very over-optimism voiced in *Renunciations of War*, in chapters[138] dealing with threats to the peace, breaches of the peace and acts of aggression, are hastening the break-down of such binding force of international law as can be expected to exist.

f. Law: Change and Self-Defence. Considering how little inclination there existed on the part of governments to bind their country by an unqualified acceptance of the jurisdiction of the International Court and how the qualifications usually nullify the acceptance in one way or another, it all seems simply a question of unwillingness, unpreparedness to do the one needful thing, a kind of primitiveness in this respect. The classification of disputes between states into 'justiciable' and 'non-justiciable' ('political') disputes, seen in this light, is a mere excuse to keep the jurisdiction of the courts restricted and the law primitive. Yet this is not the only light which can be shed on the problem, because 'the international community has not yet devised means of changing its law *pari passu* with the needs of its members'[139] and even though lawyers do not always support a rigid *status quo,* a Court (at the non-primitive level of the International Court!) 'would at this stage simply not survive many political choices of such magnitude.'[140]

This means of course that in the model of 'an international community slowly advancing towards fuller integration' such integration must proceed *on many fronts,* not only along paths which we can easily and clearly envisage, such as a stronger Court, a Police Force, a Parliament but also along paths of which we do not have an entirely valid example. With the attempts fo bring force under community

[138] Chapter VII of the Charter of the United Nations.
[139] Julius Stone, *op. cit. supra* n. 127, at 149.
[140] Julius Stone, *ibid.* note 15.

control, attempts which have been carried in some respects further in the U.N. charter than in the Pact of the League of Nations or ever before, we find that not only hopes placed on the Security Council were misconceived, but that possible means of evading community control have been left intact and perhaps been widened by adding to the 'right of self-defense' a new notion of 'collective self-defense'.[141] But the right of self-defense in the international community can by no means be equated with self-defense in antional communities (at least those which are not rent by blood-feuds) and when 'self-defense' takes place, whether justifiable or not, on a significant scale the community falls to pieces. Yet this problem does not yet seem to be amenable to any solution. In the words of Julius Stone: 'the right of self-defense under general international law is as vague as it is unquestioned, and as liable to abuse in its application as it is indispensable in the present phase of the international society'.[142] Speaking further on blue-prints for 'collective self-defense' he continues:[143] 'the use of article 51 shows itself, like that of the veto, as the frontier for the moment reached between the traditional anarchic international system, and the real collective security system projected in the charter.' This shows further, it is submitted, that Law is not an independent and self-propelling force in the international community, but is only a force when adapted to the total interplay of forces in that community. And if International Law is therefore relying as it must on, amongst other factors, the inclination of governments *under the present circumstances* to share the burdens of upholding such a law, it can not realize a project of collective security *too far ahead* of this inclination or it becomes selfdefeating — as it threatens to have become in the balance between a crumbled collective security system and a system of reconstructed (but anarchic) 'collective self-defense.' And

---

[141] Philip C. Jessup in *A Modern Law of Nations*, New York, Macmillan (1952) 163-169 thinks that 'self-defense' is circumscribed and 'collective' self-defense is not escaping the 'world authority vested in the Security Council.' The view of Julius stone, quoted below, although, or perhaps because, it leaves us more baffled, seems the better one.
[142] Julius Stone, *op. cit. supra* n. 127, Ch. IX, 'Clauses of Escape and Evasion from Peaceful Settlement and Paece Enforcement,' 242, 243.
[143] *Id.* 246.

whereas law should be to some extent utopian, and aspire to improvements, it can not therefore aspire to anything beyond a 'relevant' utopia.

6. Pacifism

a. Pacifism and Awareness. If lawyers have pinned their hopes too much on law-systems copied from local examples not comparable to the world-situation, they can be compared to most pacifists who have also anticipated a future warless world-situation and have selected possible advances towards such a warless future without envisaging all the necessary stages in such advances nor the necessary parallel developments.

One of the first steps towards the establishment of a peaceful world seems to be an awareness of its usefulness and blessings. The Romans even knew that 'dulce bellum inexpertis' ('war is something nice for people who do not know what they talk about') that is to say the 'knowing' Romans understood the value of peace. However, even the concept of the world as being ruled by reasonable men who are experienced or 'know what they talk about' seems in fact much in advance of the real situation; there are presumably more steps required for such a future than the spread of pacifist propaganda, than tales of experience.

b. Pacifism as a Propaganda. Some think therefore that 'pacifism is less a discipline than a propaganda'[144] yet is must be admitted that as a movement it has a range which includes 'learned research and publication'.[145] International Relations theory, in search for relevant models, is well advised to take cognizance of the pacifist 'steps,' whether they be 'world government,' 'international police,' 'refusal to carry arms,' 'international contact or study.' If such steps are exaggerations, they are often related somehow to real requirements, or even if they are irrelevant, it is useful to see to what extent they are so,

---

[144] Quincy Wright, *The Study of International Relations*, New York, Appleton-Century,Crofts 1953) 48.
[145] *Id.* 49.

and why, nevertheless, they exert enough fascination to enable a movement to use them as slogans.

It is submitted that the very emotionalism which surrounds these pressing questions of peace and war often obstructs the deep thinking required. It was well understood by Bernard Shaw when he refused to take part in the 'No More War Movement' of the nineteen twenties: 'I grieve to say that I don't believe in these demonstrations. People who get emotionally excited about peace are precisely the people who get excited about war . . . It is a mistake to suppose that every evil in the world can be eradicated by an article of a thousand words by me.'[146] Yet, at the same time, many peacemovements move away from elementary emotionalism and engage in research, look for new points of view, in a way which could be exemplary for scholars whose emotionalism is not less for being disguised under learned argumentation.

Further it must be understood that the pacifist's idea that 'action of some sort' is required, is probably nearer the truth than the reassuring assertion of a more contemplative kind, 'that the very existence of an international order — will bring into being processes of adaptation'.[147]

c. Pacifism: Emotion and Planning. If pacifism is in a way emotionally conditioned, as it well may be, this does not necessarily mean that it is any worse than the more pessimistic 'realism' which is also, it is submitted, to no small extent emotionally conditioned. It seems impossible to say, whether the human race is at all capable of establishing and maintaining a peaceful way of living, which will last for a very long period and will extend over at least the greater part of the surface of the earth. Not all anthropological evidence points towards bellicosity as a universal trait.[148]

It depends to some extent on the total personality whether someone tends to believe in the possibilities of pacifism *in abstracto*. For to do

[146] Quoted from Fenner Brockway, *Inside the Left*, London, George Allen & Unwin (1942) 135.
[147] R. M. MacIver, *The Web of Government*, New York, Macmillan (1947) 399.
[148] Cf. Ragnar Numeling, *The Beginnings of Diplomacy*. Copenhagen, Munksgaard (1950).

this it is emphatically not necessary to believe in the prevalence of peace in the near future, nor to believe in the likelihood of early successes for any particular pacifist scheme, nor, and this is important, *in the realizability of any now existing pacifist model.* Yet the intuitive inclination to search for alternative peaceful models, or peaceful utopias, rather than accepting fatalistically that past evils always must recur, seems, as long as one does not close one's eyes to unfavourable indications, a helpful attitude in the search for 'relevant' models in International Relations theory.

CHAPTER IV

LATER ATTEMPTS AT A MORE EXHAUSTIVE TREATMENT OF INTERNATIONAL RELATIONS

It is rather arbitrary to make any divisions between the older branches of study, which gradually discovered, so to speak, that the subject of International Relations had out-grown their domain and those more recent branches of study which, to justify their claim to universality, had partly to deal with international problems and gradually with the complete subject of International Relations. Such historical or conceptual justification as can be adduced for making nevertheless a theoretical distinction to that effect, should not disguise the inherent overlapping irregularities of theory-development and the gross oversimplifications of any attempt at systematization. The justification is often an excuse thought out afterwards. However this may be, we should not in any case become the slave of our divisions, nor of the conventional divisions made in the branches of Social Science.

1. Economics

a. Economics and Human Behaviour. The 'ancient newcomer' among the social sciences, political economy or 'macro-economic' thought makes very clear the absolute necessity of making abstract and analytical divisions of human behaviour, because observation without such divisions does not yield workable categories. Yet the development of economic science proves equally well that the abstraction has only an extremely limited validity. The better the explanation for one kind of human behaviour, the less it explains some kind of behaviour. With good reason some classical economists were happy to have found an acceptable explanation for the difference between 'value in use' and 'value in exchange' can be enhanced by productive labour or by defining 'capital' as, in some cases at least, 'accumulated labour.' But with equal reason it could, and has been argued by economists themselves, that the abstractions missed the point. 'Almost be-

fore the ink was dry on Ricardo's 'Principles,' Sismondi complained
that economic science — is so speculative that it seems divorced from
all practive —'.[149]

It is generally agreed that economic science is essentially probing
into the problem of scarcity of means and the conflicts around this
problem. 'We have neither eternal life nor unlimited means of gratification. Everywhere we turn, if we choose one thing we must relinquish others which, in different circumstances, we would not have re-
lingquished. Scarcity of means to satisfy given ends is an almost ubiquitous condition of human behaviour'.[150] This is true of the human
situation but the solution which economic science can propose to this
problem of ubiquitous scarcity of means only holds good when the
'set of circumstances' for which the solution is proposed does not
change. For that reason, economic science is often 'short-sighted' even
in the national or local sphere and certainly so in the international
sphere. For instance abundant means may become scarce or scarce
means abundant or we may not be aware that we are addicted to spu-
rious gratifications which bring us ruin instead of real satisfaction.

Moreover some economists and certainly people with a limited economic schooling have assumed that mankind surely does at all times
endeavour to preserve scarce means or to preserve goods they have
acquired with great toil. These assumptions are patently untrue.
Schemes for international cooperation based merely on the assumption
that all parties will benefit from greater economic security or will
have a greater fund of means at their disposal, do not allow for the
need to allay hidden fears, the need to acquire non-material means
for gratification, such as the desire to atone and mortify the gods, the
aspirations for friendship, respect, national or racial belonging. Ostentatious showing off, as evidenced in the highly 'uneconomic' 'pot-
latch' of primitive societies[151] as well as in 'affluent' societies.'[152] indi-

[149] Walter A. Weisskopf, *The Psychology of Economics*, University of Chicago
Press (1955) 3.
[150] Lionel Robbins, *An Essay on the Nature and Significance of Economic Science*,
London, Macmillan & Co. (1932) (2 ed. 1949) 15.
[151] W. G. Summer and A. G. Keller, *The Science of Society*, Yale University Press
(1927) Vol. 1, 263ff.
[152] Galbraith, *op. cit. supra* n. 92.

cate that economic *behaviour* is much less ubiquitous than the economic situation.

Any economic model of behaviour leads to the disquieting question, justly posed by Elton Mayo: '*must we conslude that economics is a study of human behaviour in non-normal situations, or alternatively, a study of non-normal human behaviour in ordinary situations?*'[153]

b. Economics and Sociology. The science of economics may fail to indicate how many conflicts there are in social life which are *not* about scarce goods at all. When conflicts other than those caused by the scarcity of goods bring people and groups into opposition, the model of the 'homo economicus' becomes a dismal farce. In the phenomenon of war or the apprehensiveness of war we have an bovious example where people do not attempt to preserve all categories of scarce goods, where they try to destroy goods not only of the enemy but occasionally of their own spite the enemy.

More generally: a country which would regulate its economy only on the basis of efficient production of scarce means would indulge in mono-cultures, but instead of that security-factors are continuously considered because no one dares to 'pre-suppose that we live in a peaceful and sane world.'[154] It is submitted that economists have usually underrated the 'need-to-allay-fears' as a want claiming a high ranking order of satisfaction. Part of the difficulty here is the incalculability of this need, in that it results not only in more or less logical action, such as hoarding, but also in apparently contradictory action such as simultaneous demands for disarmament conferences and for arms stock-piling. In any case the adequate valuaton of 'anxiety-needs' in the ranking order of consumer-wants is both extremely difficult and highly speculative.

It further makes economic science more and more an integral part of, if not equivalent to, socyology.

---

[153] Elton Mayo, *The Social Problems of an Industrial Civilization*, Harvard Univ. Press (1945) Ch. II: 'The Rabble Hypothesis and Its Corollary, the State Absolute' 43 (italics in the original).
[154] Hjalmar Nordfelt in *Food and Agriculture, Journal of F.A.O.* No. 2 (July-December 1947) 10.

c. Economics and the Market-Concept. Modern economists do, indeed, consider their science as simply scientific observation of human behaviour, stressing of course the behaviour connected with exchange of goods and services and influenced by market situations. They do not hesitate to make a survey of mainly economic problems within the frame-work of a generalized social science and they are prepared to entitle their work accordingly, using titles such as 'Human Action'[155] and 'International Order.'[156]

The liberal authors in this vein often stress that we must dare to see the world as a 'unit,' as having 'attained the unity of the market place.'[157] However, this is a somewhat simplified and dangerous 'model' of world affairs. It does not enlighten us about what happens insuch a vast unsurveyeable market-place. In our mind we may picture perhaps a mediaeval market-place, a totally inadequate image.

Markets can be held in communities with some sort of established order, some organization and some recognized rules. Those old-fashioned liberal protagonists of a 'free world market,' especially those referred to above, object with an amazingly childish simplicity to all the elementary requirements of the welfare principle' which according to their naive opinion[158] spoil the undiluted blessings of the 'market principle'. They fail to see that a market-place without protection of the weak, education of the innocent and prevention of fraud and seductive persuasion, turns into a slaughter-house. Apart from the need to organize and regulate a market it may be necessary to *divide*[159] the 'world'-market into surveyeable sections, into sections which serve regions held together by cultural or historical ties.

---

[155] Ludwig von Mises, *Human Action, A Treatise on Economics,* Yale Univ. Press (1949).
[156] Wilhelm Röpke, *Internationale Ordnung,* Zürich, Eugen Reutsch (1945) the previous book in his 'Trilogy' being *'Civitas Humana.'*
[157] Salvador de Madriage, *The World's Design,* London, George Allen & Unwin (1938)
[158] Ludwig von Mises, *op. cit., XVI.,* Ch. XXXV 829ff. and *passim.*
Wilhelm Röpke, *op. cit.,* Die Liberale Lösung 128ff.
[159] I have suggested that the interdependence of the local markets cannot be adjusted on a worldwide scale without 'sluicegates,' that is to say planned interference, Research for Peace, *op. cit., supra* n. 12 at 213, see also infra sub e.

d. Economics and the Market Fallacy. Apart from the above objections, I would say that in the international sphere the 'market principle' has other disadvantages, especially on the supra-economic level. The 'market principle' may be tolerably efficient in some classical wellknown examples where the market-goers belonged to a homogenous community, with desires and ideals in common, with sufficient awareness of the market-position and sufficient economic strenght, foresight and sense to postpone dealings to the next market day, when necessary. There must be some serious questioning whether such protective and comprehensible conditions prevail in the 'worldmarket.' Some of these problems we met already under the heading of geographic analysis (see *supra* Ch. III, 3, *b*). Some other problems arising out of conflicting economic-strategic assumptions, will be discussed in the next subsection (*e*). Here I must mention that most Marxist discussions of the problem not only stress objections to the 'free' market system which in my previous submission are perfectly valid, but also claim that Marxist theory has found the solution: by avoiding the capitalist system, profit making, private capital and all that, and embracing a socialist system, with no 'competitive gain and competitive spending'[160] they have discovered the proper model for a world economy.

It is submitted that this Marxist model for International Relations is a double oversimplification: it is difficult to assert that for all problems — in all periods of history! — of international concern 'the fundamental cause lies in the system of capitalist exploitation itself.'[161] Assuming further that some kinds of exploitation were indeed a contributory cause to international troubles (an assumption which is indeed convincing enough and which is valid for *some*, but not all, problems of colonialism) even then it does not follow, as most Marxists seem to imply, that with a change-over to socialist organization, *all* solutions will have been attained. Yet e.g. Prof. Bernal, a researcher in Crystallography rather than in Economics, but a Marxist with outspoken communist sympathies, is cautious enough to propose — in

---

[160] Thorstein Veblen, *An Inquiry into Nature of Peace and the Terms of its Perpetuation*, New York, Macmillan (1917) 367.
[161] J. D. Bernal asserts this in *World Without War*, London, Rutledge & Kegan Paul (1958) 106.

even flexible exchange rates[167]) or the beginnings of a tentative har-
addition to his personal belief in the 'automatic' solution[162] — concrete steps to change the world's existing 'market' with some ten or so
major industrial centres, each around a more or less autonomous base,
to an expanded and guided market with about thirty five major centres[163]. Having coupled these sensible proposals with his rigid belief
that only a socialist system will adopt them, he admits that perhaps
'far more effort will be needed by the peoples of the capitalist countries to secure this end, and that in doing so capitalism itself will be
changed out of all recognition'.[164]

It seems true enough that the free markets everywhere are corrupted by the 'supply of demand'[165] partly organized by unscrupulous
producers. However, the drastic remedy of totally 'planned demand'
is not free from pitfalls — even on a national scale — and seems as
much out of reach on a world scale as is full economic cooperation to
establish a universal world market with — in principle — a free flow
of goods.[166]

e. Economics and a Plurality of Markets. The Economic view-point
of International Relations as now generally accepted, may be best
summarized as: a collection of unharmonized but not disconnected
markets, some of which are tentatively joined, some of which are an-
tagonistic in structure or (sometimes *and*) purpose, some of which are
not well developed, some of which are perhaps too one-sidedly developed.

The un-harmonized connections are what most textbooks on International Economics are trying to analyze, especially in cases where
either the rudiments of a one-time greater harmony (movement of
migrants, or at least goods and money, fixed exchange rates, perhaps

---

[162] *Id.* 290.
[163] *Id.* 126, 127 and map at 247.
[164] *Id.* 291.
[165] Stuart Hall, 'The Supply of Demand' in *Out of Apathy* (E. P. Thompson Ed.)
London, Stevens & Sons (1960) 56-97; also of course Galbraith, *op. cit., supra* n.
92.
[166] Wilhelm Röpke speaks of 'The Fear for a World Economy' *op. cit., supra* n.
156, Par. II. This Fear is certainly not lessened by the development (since Röpke's
book in 1945) of what might called 'Federal Markets.'

mony (mutual trade,[168] pacts to that end, multilateral trade[169]) can be traced.

The 'one world-market' idea is obviously a distant utopian conception. It is even attacked as a chimerical notion, because nations, interdependent as they may be, can not indulge in any integral planning discarding national preferences.[170]

This warning against over-centralized planning, against underestimating the social *reality* of local, national[171] and regional entities, brings us nearer to the opposite end of the scale — the denial of economic- world-unity and of the 'one market' idea (whether by way of socialist 'planning' or by way of rigorous 'free' trade).[172]

It between, along this scale, we find a range of intermediate positions, some economists trying to explain what they think to be now more or less the case, some of them trying to show what should or should not be achieved.

It is admitted by all that the market of a small nation is not any longer a market by itself. It is not even a market where 'basic' industries can be established unless external trade gives an 'escape, a somewhat precarious escape' from smallness.[173]

It is admitted generally that full employment is an economic good, without which human dignity is impaired. There is no general agreement, however, regarding the possibilities of planning full em-

---

[167] John Burr Williams, *International Trade under Flexible Exchange Rates*, Amsterdam, North Holland Publishing Cy. (1954).
[168] J. E. Meade, *Trade and Welfare*, Oxford University Press (1955) Part I, II, III.
[169] *Ibid*, Part IV 499ff.
[170] Jean-Louis Fyot, *Dimensions de l'Homme et Science Economique*, Presses Universitaires de France (1952) 231: '*L'Interdépendance économique des nations s'oppose donc à une planification intégrale, dont les erreurs d'appréciation sur les besoins sociaux et les possibilités réelles de chaque nation, constitueraient un foyer de perturbations graves dans leurs échanges.*'
[171] In this sense also Jean Weiller, *Problèmes d'Economie Internationale*, Presses Universitaires de France (1950) Tome II 286.
[172] This school finds staunch, if too rigid, support from Michael A. Heilperin, *The Trade of Nations*, New York, Alfred A. Knopf (1946) 132ff. However, Heilperin admits the need of international anti-depression policies.
[173] *The Economic Consequences of the Size of Nations* (Austin Robinson, ed.), London, Macmillan & Co. (1960) XIXff. and Part IV: 247-329.

ployment, international movement of capital, products and labor; not all agree that 'trade liberalization will inevitably be stopped precisely at the point where it would lead to the progress of productivity through international changes in the location of industry.'[174] It is submitted, that this rather gloomy view is often justified and that in any case: 'in the present stage of history nations in the non-Soviet world are not prepared in peacetime to accept the degree of international human solidarity which would make possible progress towards international economic integration.'[175]

f. Economics and the Diversity of Markets. Aid to underdeveloped countries and technical assistance seem somewhat to contradict the absense of human solidarity. This aid, however, is not always planned in the real spirit of equal solidarity, although those emissionaries who head the missions are usually true apostles of development also for the less technically schooled. The very idea of 'aid' already contains a dangerous conception — international solidarity can be observed in quasi grand fashion after some provocative disaster, earthquake, floods, fires, insect-pests: foods are then shared, medicines rushed to the stricken area and volunteers flown thither. However, this never involves the abdication of a privileged position and it means only a momentary acknowledgement, in the face of nature's supreme fateful manifestation, of human equality.

In former days, even much less than a century ago, such momentary acknowledgements must also have occurred from time to time amongst owners of slaves and the factory-masters. The very condition which perpetuates or even increases existing economic cleavages prevents the distributors of occasional alms from 'joining the human race.'[176]

'International aid will fail unless it sets in motion an indigenous cumulative process of innovations and capital formation which increases productive power more rapidly than population growth.'[177] This, it is submitted, is not a plea for just increased production and sharing

---

[174] Gunnar Myrdal, *An International Economy,* New York, Harper Bros. (1956) 63.
[175] *Id.* 315.
[176] Stringfellow Barr, *Let's Join the Human Race,* University of Chicago Press (1950) and *Citizens of the World,* New York, Doubleday & Co. (1953).

the produce with the hungry areas, but it envisages that within a certain area a balance must be found, covering technique, culture, politics and economic level in an all-over picture.

With due respect to Josué de Castro, whose *Geography of Hunger*[178] contains so many useful data and remarks, in particular his insistence on a more patient study of biological processes, it is submitted that his solution is on too grand a scale and also somewhat too missionary against all attempts at population restraint.

It is not enough, for the adjustment of the world's hunger and economic pathology,[179] that the necessary means of livelihood can be produced *somewhere*, if this somewhere is in a too privileged position. Usually the whole basic philosophy of international aid is concerned with altogether different problems.[180]

In this submission extensive foreign aid *by itself*, and certainly as overwhelmingly practised at present, is not all a step towards world integration. Similarly the stepping up of international trade *by itself* is no such step towards more durable integration and the primitive conception that 'unhampered trade dovetailed with peace'[181] is totally misleading. Much muddled thinking may be retraced to insufficient appreciation of how the political and economic are simultaneous and intertwined problems where it is impossible to say whether the economic egg is really in any sense prior to the political chicken or vice versa.

g. Economics in Social Life. We have now returned to two point with which we started: *Firstly:* The economic side of life interlocked with

---

[177] Horace Belshaw, *Population Growth and Levels of Consumption*, London, George Allen & Unwin, under auspices of Institute of Pacific Relations (1956) XIX.

[178] Josué de Castro, *Geography of Hunger*, London, Victor Gollancz (1952).

[179] Seymour E. Harris, *International and Interregional Economics*, New York, McGraw-Hill (1957), Ch. 16, 'The Pathology of International Economics' 208-237.

[180] *Ibid.*

Also: Charles Wolf, Jr., *Foreign Aid, Theory and Practice in Southern Asia*, Princeton Univ. Press (1960).

[181] From the memories of Cordell Hull, criticized by Richard N. Gardner in *Sterling Dollar Diplomacy*, Oxford. Clarendon Press (1956) 9: 'In reality, of course, the failure to conclude trade agreements with the Axis Powers was a symptom, not a cuase of the bad political relations that eventually led to war.'

the political and the social.[182] They all are distinguishable but indivisible aspects of human behaviour. The study of that behaviour must necessarily include a consideration of behaviour as manifest from the point of view of International Relations; yet behaviour is so much more understandable and a proper object for study in more or less integrated communities than in the whole wide world at large, that few worthwhile observations have been made in the field of economics which are of assistance to International Relations theory. On the contrary: concern with International Relations may possibly occasion economists to pause for further thinking, perhaps for transition.[183] As eminent an economist as Kindleberger admits that 'if international economic equilibrium can be obtained only at the cost of other social goals, such as national political and social equilibrium or international peace, it is not worth while. Social scientists are only beginning to explore this subject.'[184] Whilst he believes that economists can not very well outgrow the limited terms of economic equilibrium, he does stress at the same time that 'concepts of equity cannot be eliminated from national economic life.'[185] As soon as there is a need to consider equity there is also a need 'to modify the economic goal of efficiency for this purpose.'[186]

Of course it is difficult enough in any national industry to clip, say, the wings of oversized luxury cars, let alone of a possibly oversized motorcar industry. To reach anything of the kind by international arrangement is very much more difficult and to attempt to reach it on a global scale may be utopian to the degree of irrelevance.

Secondly: I accepted the economists' model of a 'World Market' with a number of qualifications: perhaps the concept is in practice not only unwieldy but hampering to the formation of a relevant

[182] Cf., e.g., William Ashworth, *A Short History of the International Economy 1850-1950*, London, Longmans, Green & Co., (1952).

[183] Bart Landheer, *Pause for Transition*, The Hague, M. Nijhoff, (1957) 136: 'emphasis, shifted to related disciplines which take a much wider view of human nature and which may ultimately lead to a more correct analysis of human need.'

[184] Charles P. Kindleberger, *International Economics*, Homewood, Illinois, Richard D. Irwin (1953) 518.

[185] *Ibid* p. 520 (and at p. 522: 'In international trade, efficiency has stood by itself, and there has been no room for considerations of equity — At least this was the case. There is reason to think that the situation may be changing.').

ideal. Several of the most serious attempts at analysis of the world economy have made a division into regions, and have included in their analysis the prospects of growth and developments as seen for those regions.[187] It is submitted that both for the purpose of a workable survey *and* for a model to direct thought and political-economic efforts, the conception of a *plurality of markets* (centered round or co-extensive with geographical regions where industrial-agricultural balances can be realized) is more fruitful than the conception of a global World Market.

If this model is followed such centralized economic institutions as have been founded will appear rather as coordinating bodies than as institutions with a central economic-political driving force: possibly in some cases this is even correct, whilst in other cases the model needs further refinement. It needs, probably, the further division of the world into additional, yet to be created, markets as suggested by Bernal (*supra*, sub *d*). This submission however is not intended as an endorsement of Leopold Kohr's suggestion that some nations which have grown through the unification of smaller units should attempt to split up again,[188] — because, notwithstanding all the interdependence of the political and economic, the loyalties which a nation can command are stronger and less amenable to artificial surgery than are the attachment to markets and economic regions, although political interference on this level alone is obviously also fraught with difficulties and opposing loyalties.

2. Politics

a. Politics and Human Behaviour. In more than one sense Economics is a later science than the Science of Politics. Yet, as we have seen, Economics has developed into a stage at which some or most of its ultimate problems are referred back to Political Science, if not to the Social Sciences in general.

This seems a paradox; if the economic branch of thinking leads to illusory insights when the wider sociological and philosophical prob-

---

[187] Thorkil Kristensen and Associates, *The Economic World Balance*, Copenhagen, Munksgaard, (1960).
[188] Leopold Kohr, *The Breakdown of Nations*, London, Routledge & Kegan Paul (1957).

lematics of human behaviour are not re-introduced, does that not mean that economic 'specialization' was in essence a mistake?

The paradox can be pursued further: Political Science has developed to a stage at which some or most of its ultimate problems are referred back to the Psychological and Social Sciences in general.[189] Does this mean the specialization of Political Science was an aberration?

The two questions deserve much further attention. They cannot be readily answered[190] but neither can they be avoided. They seem intimately connected with our central question: what is International Relations theory attempting to do? Is *its* specialization also an aberration?

I should like to put forward two preliminary submissions from which further questions will follow. The submissions are, it is believed, generally assumed by, or at least generally acceptable to, the majortity of students of International Relations. The accompanying questions may be answered in several ways and no answer will be generally acceptable.

The first submission is that Economics and Political Science found their proper perspective only when some theoretical conclusions had to withstand the acid test of application on a world scale. (For futhar elucidation of this submission see *infra* sub *b*.). The acessory questionmark is then whether Economics and Politics are not 'formed' (or 'deformed') by their historical growth in a restricted local or national environment so as to be of little relevance to the problematics of world affairs?

The second submission is that at present the theoretical outlook in International Relations is essentially that of Political Science (for further elucidation of this submission see *infra* sub *c*.). Admittedly to

---

[189] See, e.g., Charles E. Merriam, *Systematic Politics*, Univ. of Chicago Press (1945). Daniel Lerner and Harold D. Lasswell (eds.) *The Policy Sciences*, Stanford Univ. Press (1951).

[190] It is not necessary to deny some truth in the assertion of David Easton *The Political System*, New York, Alfred A. Knopf, (1953) 100 that 'The intrinsic logic of the development is the vehicle which gave direction to the historical process of fragmentation and specialisation.'. This however does not absolve us from checking the correctness of that so-called intrinsic logic. The science of logic is far from static!

some extent the outlook is 'sociological' rather than 'political' (see *infra section 3*). The accessory question-mark is whether this politically orientated approach is basically sound and needs merely additional 'perspectives,' refinements and corrections — or is it basically misleading and in need of a complete overhaul?

b. Politics and Needs. Political theory must have had its origins in doubt and dissatisfaction,[191] even where it sings a song of praise in honour of a given political system or process.

Often such praise is originally given to a system or institution as an indirect criticism of another system or institution, but in subsequent political writing this is usually forgotten.

The acquired 'holiness' of the principle of 'the Separation of Powers' (legislative, administrative and judicial) has largely resulted from the inquisitive effort of one of the most influential political scientist of all time who, in his search for remedies against abuses in his own country, idealized what he admired in England.[192]

That Montesquieu's principal concern was a 'curative' one,[193] can be more easily demonstrated than in the case of other, but it might apply even to hard-boiled 'realists' such as Machiavelli or Hobbes, whose desire was presumably less to make their readers despondent than to show them what course to follow. In most cases Political Science has been a mixture of description and pre-scription; often the conditions described have been seen through the perspective of the intuitively conceived curative prescription.[194] though the two conceptions are not often so artfully blended as in *'De l'Esprit des Lois.'*[195]

[191] See Ch. II *supra*.
[192] Montesquieu, *De l'Esprit des Lois*, especially Book XI, Ch. VI (edition par Gonzaque Truc: Paris, Editions Garnier frères, *Classiques* Garnier; sans date). R. Kranenburg in *Political Theory*, Oxford University Press (1939) 52 thinks: 'When it comes to analysis his precision is remarkable.' However, it is not necessary to believe this at all in order to admire Montesquieu.
[193] Gonzaque Truc, *id*. VII. *'En politique il est mené par l'horreur du despotisme, en religion par celle du fanatisme.'*
[194] Cf. *Supra*, Chapter II.
[195] Cf. the very instructive remarks of Robert Dahl in his review of De Jouvenel *'La Souveraineté'*: *World Politics* II 19, 83ff. 89: 'Political Theory is stimulated more by the threat of failure...'

What concerns us most at the moment, however, is the fact that, until perhaps well into this century, the basic concern of Political Science, a concern which determined its perspective, in its descriptive as well as prescriptive aspects, was with local or national authority, power or government. It is not enough to say that the Political Science perspective was so restricted, without admitting that governmental activity and governmental 'concern' was, if not so limited, often so concentrated also. Always foreign policy has been pursued to a great extent for home consumption and there are no signs that this has changed lately or will easily change in the near future.

Authority, power and government are by no means identical, but they are related phenomena and fill the onlooker with awe, with a desire to oversome some of the terrible consequences of concentrated authority, power and government. Political Science has been mostly the attempt to 'tame' (whether intellectually or by prescribing social remedies) the absolutism of the authority-power-government process. It concerned itself with the problem of people requiring guidance and leadership but subsequently being unable to control their power-inflated guides. The International Relations perspective needs a further dimension: it is not enough for any group to work out its internal relationships and ranking order, but the way in which it does this must be compatible with the ways of other groups. The taming of governments vis-a-vis their subjects does noet help the subjects any more if the governments are not tamed vis-a-vis each other. Modern Political Science takes this 'modern problem'[196] into account. To the problems arising from this further perspective (and to some doubtful theorems in connection therewith) we must return after first considering the view that the International Relations perspective is now normally seen as an extension of Political Science and, simultaneously with this, the question whether this 'political' approach is perhaps a basic mistake.

[196] Cf. Merriam, *op. cit. supra* n. 189 Ch. x 319ff. 'The future of Government': (I) Utopias (II) The Modern Problem. And *id.* 325 ('A Jural Order of the World'): 'There cannot be free states unless there is a free world.' Admittedly this well sounding phrase may just be another aphorism — it suggests however, a deep problem to which Merriam rightly called attention and which goes far beyond the problem of 'State-Sovereignty.'

c. Politics and the International Scene. When Grayson Kirk reported in 1947 on the conference organized by the Council of Foreign Relations the year before on teaching and research in International Relations, he divided the subject matter under the broad headings of Law, Organization and Politics.[197] What International Law and International Organization are, he indicated in a few sentences; but such a succint indication would not do for International 'Politics' and although 'the student realizes that he must know something of geography, demography, economics, social psychology etc., he feels somewhat in the position of an ass in the midst of many bundles of hay.'[198]

Why, however, should he be an impudent ass and pick the bundle which is the most elusive and of such 'exasperating complexity?'[199] The most readily available answer is: 'all the other asses do it too.' If we take the majority of the books published on the subject or if we recall the name of one of the best, if not the very best journal dealing with the subject, we find the same emphasis on politics, on 'World Politics'.

There is also an answer as to the heart of the matter: International Relations theory must be interested in the way *decisions are arrived at,* by whom, on what 'authority,' with what effect and with what degree of resignation on the part of those who are or may be affected by the decisions.

These decisions are (as I have tried to show) not the only important element to be taken in account in order to understand what happens in International Relations. On the contrary a full and extensive enumeration of all political decisions by statesmen, diplomats, military and civil leaders all over the globe (an enumeration such as may be regularly compiled in yearbooks and chronicles) does not increase insight without some further relatedness — on the level of the 'decisions' or 'resolutions' as reported as well as on the level of external and background factors. Even if we should adopt the exaggerated view of Tolstoy and his division of the world's statesmen (as he divided army-commanders) into crazy, dashing Napoleons whose many

---

[197] Grayson Kirk, *The Study of International Relations in American Colleges and Universities,* New York, Council on Foreign Relations (1947) 9.
[198] *Id.* 10.
[199] *Id.* 21.

plans and initiatives come to naught as against wise phlegmatic Kuzu-
tovs whose plans follow the stream of events, yet we have to realise
that inactivity is a form of decision and it is the *decision* in each case,
the wisdom of it and also the fixing of authority and responsibility for
taking it (or for not taking it) which make up the subject of Political
Science, In the national sphere Political Science has compared the
ends or goals of Government with the formal organizational authority (who is allowed to decide what?) and with the intrinsic processes
by which authority was gained and exercised, the 'tools of Government,'[200] or 'who gets what, when, how?'[201]

Prime Ministers, Foreign Minsters, Party Leaders, Business Execu-
tives, Propagandists have a role in World Affairs about which the
same general, non-precise submission can be made as was put forward
in Ch. III, section 2 about Diplomats, namely: that they are not altogether irrelevant to the constellation in which they act but that their
personal behaviour can only have a very limited effect on that constellation. Yet the very admission that personal effort can have some
effect, that even some little scope for individuals in certain positions
exists, links any scientific analysis of the constellation to Political
Science.

d. Politics and Decision-Making. The previous submission has been so
un-specific, so non-committal, so 'slippery,' that one would like to
catch the exact *moment where the decision becomes,* in stead of
vaguely 'not irrelevant,' *really decisive.* Attempts have indeed been
made to redefine 'Politics,' for the purpose of making it more fit to
use as 'an approach' (not '*the*' approach!) to the study of International Relations.

One such attempt is the proposal by Richard C. Snyder and his associates[202] to expand the study of 'Decision-Making' to such extent
that all the information (or lack of it) at the disposal of every deci-
sion-maker, every possible alternative choice or strategy, every one of

---

[200] Merriam, *op. cit. supra* n. 189.
[201] Harold Lasswell, *Politics, Who Gets What, When, How?* New York, McGraw
Hill (1936), Meridian ed. (1958).
[202] Richard C. Snyder, Hw. Bruck, and Burton Sapin, 'Decision-Making as an Approach to the Study of International Politics,' *Foreign Policy Analysis Project Series No. 3,* Princeton (1954).

his perceptions (including the mistaken prejudices 'traceable to bu-
reaucratic pathology') can be really caught in an intellectual 'trap' so
to say, or as Hoffmann puts it, in one of the 'smaller boxes' with
which 'the box built by Mr. Snyder is filled.'[203]

It is submitted that the Snyder approach, although making the decision-making process and the decision-makers central and sovereign,
and making political processes like other social processes ('opinion
formation') subordinate and/or contributory thereto, is really an extended political approach. It is further submitted that the undesirable
vagueness of the Political Science assumption (decisions influence the
constellation to some extent but are influenced to some extent by the
constellation) is reduced by Snyder but not overcome. Probably this is
so because some measure of vagueness is inescapable. Criticism of
Snyder, like the one levelled by Hoffmann, on the ground that room
for vagueness has not been eliminated is not quite fair,[204] but it is
probably correct that the extended approach is leading us to an over-
detailed approach; 'it is impressive as a detailed approach to the study
of decision-making, not to the whole of international relations.'[205]

Hoffmann compares this over-detailed approach with the simpler
and more convincing framework in Bernard Cohen, *The Political
Process and Foreign Policy* (Princeton 1957). This I have not done.
On the other hand I was impressed by Richard Snyder's own broader
treatment of the decision-making process (on who is deciding, what
the motivations and personality-influence are) in his analysis of
American Foreign Policy.[206]

[203] Stanley N. Hoffman, *op. cit. supra* n. 23 at 52. Of the Monograph itself a selected reading is given *id.* 150-165.
[204] Says Hoffmann, *ibid:* 'One of the paradoxes of the search for pure 'interrelat-
edness' is that the scheme ends with a mere enumeration of factors: we are being
shown the pearls, and we are told that they somehow connected'. However, real
pearls — certainly of this kind — can be strung more than one way.
[205] Hoffmann, *id.* 53.
[206] Edgar S. Furniss and Richard C. Snyder, *American Foreign Policy*, New York,
Rhinehart & Co. (1945-1959) 89-118. Attention may be drawn to Walter J. H.
Sprott's insistence, from the sociological-political view, that the moods, ideas and
perceptions of 'The Policy Makers' differ from those of the scientists. Paper at
Liege Congress (1953) of the International Sociological Association. ISA-
L-IC-Int-70.

It is likely therefore that a line must be drawn where analysis of decision-making becomes futile for International Relations Theory.

e. Politics and Conflict. Another attempt to escape a vague indetermination (between 'political activity' and the international situation) is the reverse of Snyder's sociological extension and exists in a rigid sociological restriction of all 'international politics' to 'oppositional relations of groups,'[207] Quincy Wright goes so far as to say 'once an end is achieved, as in the passage of legislation, or once an opinion comes to be accepted by practically everyone, as is true of much of science, oppositions may die out and the end will cease to be political.' Whatever Quincy Wright has to say on our subject deserves respectful consideration and, moreover, in his preface[208] he justifies his restricted definition of the term 'international politics' as being necessary in order to *distinguish* it from the 'whole' of International Relations on the one hand and from the normal (non-international) Political Science departments on the other hand. Moreover this exact definition proved its usefulness when Prof. Wright showed how problems of 'world stabilization' or of 'stability and progress' could be conceived and analyzed.[209] Nevertheless it is submitted — with some diffidence — that rigid adherence to a definition of the political as 'the organizing for controversy' may be undesirable.

It is necessary indeed to recognise the hidden controversies where they exist but do not always appear at the surface. In this sense the political is indeed related to such phenomena as a mere 'shadow'-opposition, a 'potential' or 'imagined' opposition, potential rather than real. On the other hand the political relates to a division or allocation[210] of authority or a choice made by universal acclaim. Does the

---

[207] Quincy Wright, *The Study of International Relations*, New York, Appleton-Century-Croft (1955) 131.

[208] *Id.* ix.

[209] See: Quincy Wright, *Problems of Stability and Progress in International Relations.* University of California Press (1954). I am grateful to Prof. Wright for a very helpful and suggestive letter on all these problems when I had asked his advice whilst re-writing the above section.

[210] This element of allocation, whether it be personnel to roles or facilities to personnel is suggestively discussed by Talcott Parsons, *The Social System*, Glencoe, The Free Press (1952) 114ff.

end then cease to be political? An opposition postponed, possibly not at all organized but smouldering, could be thought to make even temporary agreements political, but there is another aspect of greater importance.

Politics seem to me to be more than the organizing of oppositions as for a final trial of strength. Often it seems rather the organized *avoidance* of such a trial, whether by accomodation or by shifting the onus of choice to a recognized authority. The 'manipulation of consent' would, admittedly, still fall under Prof. Wright's definition, but a narrow definition would not emphasize sufficiently the role of the legal, the ethical and the *renunciation* of opposition within the political. All these factors are so intimately intertwined that frontier-lines are blurred, and insight is not gained by overprecision.

A political decision need not be based on a virtual counting of votes or calculation of support. Acuiescence is often obtained — notwithstanding the clamour of strong opposition — when the 'justice' of a decision is resolutely asserted.

It is often held that a precise definition of politics — when scientifically adhered to — is always better than vague terminology; yet it may be highly misleading to attempt to simplify the widespread — rough and unscientific — notion of International Politics to one clear-cut aspect thereof ('the controversy') by way of a sharp definition.

For the time being the theory of International Relations has, it is submitted, not yet reached the stage where general elusiveness can be avoided through refined definitions with limited applicability.

f. Politics: Roles and Fears. Behind the 'decision-making' approach and the 'conflict-organization' approach a deeper sociological-political dilemma of alternative analytical approaches appears: must society, or its political systems, be analyzed according to the personality-types which characterize groups and their leaders or 'elites': or should it be analyzed according to 'positions,' types of organization and association. When reverting hereafter (sub 3) to the sociological theories and hypotheses of International Relations these two distinguishable kinds of approach will again become manifest.

This is a crucial dilemma for International Relations theory and, it is submitted, very little has been done even to pose the dilemma in a proper way.[211] It seems that the true believers in the decisionmaking approach overestimate the importance of their heros and villains and that the true believers in the powers of a 'system' overestimate the benefits, or the curses, which a 'system' can bestow or the rigidity with which a 'role' in a system is (*necessarily* as they think) acted. However unpleasant it is for theorists to admit such wavering vagueness, it does not seem possible to say more than that there exists *some* relatedness between a political system and the roles to be acted by the representatives in such system and that this relatedness cannot be defined with more than a rough approximation.

In order to analyze any relatedness it must be proved first however, that a role-player is actually 'caught' in a system and it seems that, particularly in International Relations theory, all too often a 'system of thought,' perhaps better called a 'mode of thought,' is called a 'system of forces' or a 'balance of power.' It is submitted that much confusion has been occasioned not only by not admitting a parial indeterminedness (between international role-players and international systems in which they play) but even more so by *elevating the speculations and apprehensions of politicians* (about the interplay of forces) with which they must, or think they must, reckon) to something other than their subjective system of calculation, namely to a quasi-objective basic constellation (under the terms of 'functioning forces' or 'equilibrium'[212]).

It is submitted that the 'Balance of Power' should be understood as a 'Balance of Fears and Apprehensions,' that the whole conception

[211] For the Social Sciences in general the problem is, of course, not a new one. It is implicit in the difference in stress between the social-psychological approach and sociological approach. See Talcott Parsons, *id.* 31. In International Relations theory both stresses may be, in fact, equally relevant.

[212] George Liska, *International Equilibrium,* Harvard University Press (1957) concluding chapter 187ff. I think the magic word of 'equilibrium' tends to become abused in political and sociological theory altogether. It explains very little. Moreover: 'Our world is full of crises — conditioned, imperfectly structured relationships among persons and collectivities; under such conditions of rapid and massive change that we may require ideas more novel than 'equilibrium' to understand them'. Robin M. Williams Jr. 'Continuity and Change in Sociological Study' (1958), *American Sociological Review* 629, 630.

makes no sense other than as a corollary of aggression and conquest and their anticipation. For that reason, it is further submitted, the anxiety which, in anticipation of such aggression, leads to attempts to 'balance' the powers should be analyzed as an anxiety-state at high altitude — precipitating the vertigo (the 'defensive' wars) it attempts to avoid[213] — rather than as an objective interplay of forces.

g. Politics and Systematic Analysis. In connection with the submission that the 'Balance of Powers' is not more than a system of tactical thinking, and not a 'positional system,' reference may be made to Morton Kaplan's attempt to bring 'systematic theory' in the analysis of international politics.[214] Perhaps the critical description of this step by Hoffmann[215] as 'a huge misstep in the right direction' has found wider acclaim than even Morton Kaplan's book and its attempts to re-organize analytical theory. I must admit that I have not been able to determine what systems and what processes we can, on Mr. Kaplan's advice, select, or what 'sub-systems' we could extract from the international scene (which Kaplan thinks is not a political 'system'). I do believe, however, that this vagueness is not merely or mainly because of his over-complicated language, but because of the intrinsic vagueness (see sub 4 and 5 supra) of the recognizable factors in international decision-making and situations, and the further vagueness of their mutual inter-relatedness, so that rigidly precise theory becomes inappropriate. However, Mr. Kaplan is unwilling to accept vagueness philosophically. Yet his full inventory of alternatives is, it is submitted, of doubtful use, not only for the predictive purposes which their author mentions as a future hope, but even for the purpose of gaining a more general insight and understanding. If we had a much more concrete knowledge of the facts which *are indeed* (and not merely 'could be' hypothetically) at the basis of the abstract 'roles' tentatively outlined by Kaplan, his theory would lose much of its

[213] I have stated this prosposition: 'The Balance of Powers is but a balance of fears' explicitly in 'The Influence of Anxiety and Fear on International Relations,' *Law and Economics*, Vol. IV. no. IV (June 1958), Published by Tel-Aviv University.
[214] Morton Kaplan, *System and Process in International Politics*, New York, John Wiley & Sons (1957) XI.
[215] Stanley H. Hoffman, *op. cit. Supra* n. 23 at 40.

ambiguity. That is true enough; but at that very moment we would not need the kind os theoretical choice-indications towards which Kaplan has attempted to guide us.

h. Politics and Expectations. Argument in Political Science has often been coloured by the 'curative design' or by a somewhat related design of 'commendation' or 'reprobation.' Derogatory statements about human character have acquired the stamp of immutable wisdom, because these statements always contained warnings against the concentration of 'power' in the hands of a few — and history has shown, and probably always will show, the dangers of the abuse of power.

Why have so few political scientists dared to utter a more benevolent and optimistic judgement? If it is true that power corrupts and absolute power corrupts absolutely — as is often the case — it is also true that power conveys a sense of responsibility, that, often, a man rises to the occasion.

Here is an outstanding problem for theory in politics and, it is submitted, few have probed it with such keen insight as R. H. S. Crossman, probably because he combined the qualities of a scholar with the experience (and not always a frustated experience, which is noteworthy) of a politician. His comparison[216] of Locke — the more practical, the more understanding and now also the more 'dated' of the two — and Hobbes — the less experienced but the asker of more funadmental questions and the maker of more ultimate guesses as to why peaceful citizens accept murderous leaders — is of eminent interest to students of politics in general and of international politics in particular. It is the problem that a political system must be run by people who really 'run' it, that is to say who also can 'abuse' their facilities. There may be some safeguard in election or control, but, as the Roman satirist[217] might well ask: 'who is to guard the guards themselves?'

Over-democratic democrats make assumptions which not only can never be proved, but which in some cases may be patently untrue.

216 R. H. S. Crossmann, *Government and the Governed*, London, Christophers (1939) 54-80.
217 Decimus Junius Juvenalis, *Satires* VI, 347.

They assume that the democratic 'system,' that is a system with extensive procedures for all the possible safeguards in electing, checking and ejecting leaders (with the approval of some sort of majority of the governed) necessarily produces leaders with a greater concern for and understanding of the needs of the governed than leaders who emerge by less respectable methods.

In the first place it is an unproved assumption that the electorate itself understands its needs or, if so gifted, would endure a long series of unpopular measures for the sake of those needs alone if given a choice to adopt less beneficial but more agreeable measures. Nor can it be proved that an authoritarian leader could not act with a high sense of reponsibility and a keen insight in the needs of those he leads.

Some of the specific problems of the 'conduct of foreign relations' by democratic governments have been posed by Alexis de Tocqueville over a century ago, systematically studied and analyzed by De Witt C. Poole over a quarter century ago[218] and recently reconsidered in a most important and intelligent survey by Max Beloff.[219] This last survey is full of critical remarks which need attentive thought — such as the submission that *some* of the problems of foreign policy are *indentical* for democracies and totalitarian states,[220] that the *ignorance* of the electorate is not the only or most serious problem but one which must be seen in relation to the electorate's *false expectations*,[221] that much 'democratic' *reporting* is tuned to the public expectation and for all its semblance of objectivity is nevertheless false or misleading.[222]

i. Politics and Improvement. It is well known that the study of political behaviour must survey potential talent, intellectuality, morality and its perversion as well as actual performance in past practice.

---

[218] De Witt C. Poole, *The Conduct of Foreign Relations under Modern Democratic Conditions,* Yale University Press (1924).

[219] Max Beloff, *Foreign Policy and the Democratic Process,* Baltimore, John Hopkins Press (1955).

[220] *Id.* 17.

[221] *Id.* 48-55.

[222] *Id.* 91-92. Cf. J. Barents, *Democracy: An Unagonized Re-appraisal,* The Hague, Van Keulen (1958) 44-46.

Since this has been done already so often in most political writing no dramatic new wisdom is likely to be forthcoming.[223] Such a study requires insight into 'performance' as much as into 'system.' In this respect the study of democracy has to pay attention at least as much to the prevalence of tolerance on the part of the majority towards the minority, as to the electoral or constitutional safeguards.

It is, however, also submitted that present-day political scientists have a tendency to over-stress the weaknesses and follies of human nature. This is probably so because only at the beginning of this century[224] were these negative aspects adequately pointed out for further thinking. This notwithstanding, and in spite of the obvious risks involved in any system whatsoever, particularly in a system which puts optimistic expectations so high as to invite bitter disappointments, it is more useful for political science to search for instances of reasonable political adequacy, and to analyze the contributory factors, than to concentrate on the most blatant cases of failure. This hopeful approach is, however, justified only, when not coupled to the assumption that there exists already, or there has ever existed a fully developed, wise, tolerant political system which could cope with more than the most simple and locally restricted problems.

j. Politics and the Social Sciences. Political Science is never the last word of wisdom. It refers back to psychology,[225] to sociology (probably more than to any other discipline), to philosophy and to economics — perhaps as much as economics refers to political science.[226] Sociology is such a wide term that some more restricted term like Political Sociology or Sociology of Political Behaviour indicates a proper field for study.

We now must revert to our earlier question: is the political ap-

---

[223] The compact but far from superficial survey by D. E. Butler, *The Study of Political Behaviour*, Hutchinson, 2nd ed. (1959) 101ff. comes to practically the same conclusion.

[224] Cf. Graham Wallas, *Human Nature in Politics*, London, Contable (1908).

[225] H. J. Eysenck, *The Psychology of Politics*, London, Routledge & Kegan Paul (1954).

[226] Douglas V. Verney, *The Analysis of Political Systems*, London, Routledge & Kegan Paul (1959) 230.

proach to International Relations also a 'huge misstep in the right direction' and would it be better to study the subject mainly from the sociological angle?

Part of the answer is supplied by the extension of political science towards the background phenomena of political decisions, environments, action and the so called 'feedback' of all these phenomena.[227] Political Scientists are therefore looking beyond the traditional subdivisions of political study: goals, interest and means. Also beyond decision-making, power, and governmental authority.

The sociological study of International Relations, including the psychological, covers even wider relevant topics such as prejudice, conflict-strategy in the abstract, national character and culture.

Will sociology eventually tell us that a political decision is never a *free* decision, that the politicians are not more than the marionettes in a ballet of death — the model we considered, and rejected, for diplomats?

Again the submission is: to some extent political behaviour in the international sphere is pre-ordained by the situation and yet to some extent behaviour, which is a wider notion than decision or action, does influence the situation. It is not a very satisfactory guiding-line, it is too vague and too hesitant, but it points inescapably to the overriding importance of Political Science for the theory of International Relations.

3. Sociology

a. Sociology leaves Gaps of Knowledge. The sociological approach to International Relations seems more inclusive than any previously mentioned approach and for that reason might be considered to be more informative and safer to follow.

I would argue however that the all-inclusiveness — in principle — of Sociology is neither safe nor all-informative, for the reason that sociological analysis of necessity must be selective, and selection not only necessarily involves omission but may very well involve the

---

[227] For a useful discussion see Joseph Frankel, 'Towards a Decision Making Model in Foreign Policy,' *Political Studies*, Vol. VII, no. 1 (Feb. 1959) p. 1ff.

omission of very important, if not the most important aspects of what we should know.

I would further submit that sociological analysis of International Relations is focussed, much like Political Science or, for that matter, Medicine, on the pathological side of the problems studied.

Whether we take the 'psycho-sociological' approach, embodied in particular in the UNESCO-sponsored 'tensions-research' or the more 'position-centered' analysis, embodied in particular in the kind of 'conflict-research' prosposed by Jessie Bernard (to mention ist most pronounced representative), it is clear that these two most important streams of sociological theory in the field of International Relations both lead to a concentrated attention on conflict and war.[228]

Conflict and war are not a sufficient 'extract' of International Relations and the search for means of avoiding conflict and war, as long as it is so narrowly limited and concentrated, will probably not yield the means sought and searched for.

In this connection I would argue moreover that the sociological search for means to avoid or solve conflict in the international sphere is unduly influenced by the successes of industrial sociology.

The first of the submissions, that of sociological 'omissions' and lack of safety, needs little comment in view of the theoretical assumptions submitted in Ch. II. Some comment however (see below *b*) will be given on the kinds of 'explanation' given by Sociology.

The other submission is to be elucidated in the light of the psycho-sociological and the positional-conflict models used for the analysis of international strife. (See infra *c* and *d*).

b. Sociology and Explanation. Sociology attempts to explain in general what History has described in particular. No one has demonstrated with greater clarity than William Dray, what are the fallacies and pitfalls of so called historical explanation.[229]

---

[228] These two streams are competently summarized in *The Nature of Conflict*, ed. by Jessie Bernard, T. H. Pear, Raymond Aron, Robert C. Angell, Paris, UNESCO (1957). Cf. the present writer's review in *Journal of Conflict Resolution* Vol. II No. 2 (June 1958).

[229] William Dray, *Laws and Explanation in History*, London, Oxford University Press (1957).

In the first place Dray shows (following others who have, however, not been so precise) that historical exposition assumes constant logical or causal corollaries. Its record is written in such a way that these exact causalities are often tacitly assumed, as 'covering laws,' when a certain event is said to follow necessarily from another event. A big army defeats a small one, a clever general beats a stupid one, a cruel ruler is murdered: the events seem to need no further explanation. At least not until refinements are needed, as when the big army gets demoralized or the clever general lacks equipment or the well-guarded cruel ruler succeeds in dying in bed without the aid of a murderer.

Dray however 'explains' explanation further than by intellectually unraveling the 'covering laws' and their sub-laws: by showing that in some cases the explanation is fully causal and in other cases it is not more than 'making familiar,' showing how the corollary has occurred elsewhere. If it is true that in historical explanation these two kinds of explanation are not only thoroughly confused but often indistinguishable, then the same, it is submitted, applies to a great deal of sociological explanation. Probably more so, because historical events lend themselves more readily to painstaking analysis than the more speculative conjectures used in sociology. True enough, in smaller groups the sociological conjectures can be subjected, to some extent, to tests and controls, but the larger the group or tre set of groups involved, the more difficult is it to render speculative conjecture into probable conjecture or to render the latter into proposed trends which may be safely assumed.

At this stage it is important to remember that we judge 'explanation' by a mixture of 'reasonableness' (or familarity) and 'predictive adequacy' and that (see Ch. II, section 7) neither are fool-proof evidence for the correctness of the explanation. Logical explanation is of course absolutely valid only for logically defined categories, as in mathematics or formal logic, but logical explanation in the social sciences, which exists and which is valuable enough, is valid only to the extent that the abstractions used are relevant and then only for the time they remain relevant.

On account of the complexity and fluidity of the situations involved, it is submitted that sociological explanation in international affairs can never be more than approximate and speculative, that is to say that the use of 'covering laws' is not much more than just 'familiarizing.'

c. Sociology of Tensions. What is loosely called the 'UNESO-Tensions Research' is based on two conjectures, one of which seems undeniable, but the second of which does not at all necessarily follow from the first.

Much research[230] has been done to bring to light the prevalence of stereotyped thinking and the rigid images in respect of nationality, of foreigners, friends and enemies.

It is important for International Relations theory to follow this analysis of the phenomenon of 'national character,' which appears to be illusory to a great extent, though perhaps not altogether.[231]

It may be surmised that many politicians and that even many scientific researchers at Foreign Office desks as well as many military experts have been fooled by their own prejudices or by notions which were dated, if ever applicable.

Yet it should *not* be surmised, as may erroneously have been done by much UNESO-Tensions-Research, that the illusory thinking as such can explain all conflict and, in the end, even the phenomenon of war.

d. Sociology of Rational Conflict. The reaction against the over-emphasis on 'tensions' as a source of conflict has been neatly formulated

---

[230] *Tensions Affecting International Understanding,* Otto Klineberg, (ed.) New York, Social Science Research Council (1950).
'National Stereotypes and International Understanding,' *International Social Science Bulletin,* (Autumn 1951) Vol. III, no. 3. *The Nature of Conflict* (Jessie Bernard *et al,* eds.) Paris, UNESCO (1957).
[231] H. C. J. Duyker and N. H. Fryda, *National Character and National Stereotypes,* Amsterdam, North Holland Publishing Co. (1960).
Burkart Holzner, *Völkerspychologie,* Würzburg, Holzner Verlag, no date (ca. 1960).
Handbook of Social Psychology (ed. Gardner Lindzey), Reading, Mass. Addison Wesly Publishing Co. (1954), Ch. 26; 'National Character' by Alex Inkeles and Daniel J. Levinson.

by Jessie Bernard: 'Do the politicies reflect the tensions or do the tensions reflect the policies?'[232]

In some cases it has been reasonably demonstrated that the conflict engendered the stereotyped thinking, as in the case of the Korean conflict, where increasingly unfavourable views of the Russians were held by Americans *following* rather than preceding the political 'tension' (in the sense of conflict)[223].

Yet, I would say that the model of an objective inexorable conflict-situation, which means the existence of social conditions leading always to a perfectly rational conflict, regardless of stereotyped thinking, is a model — used by Bernard and Abel[234] and to a great extent by 'Game-Theorists' — far removed from reality.

In the first place the 'rationality' of the decision to fight a conflict out, to go to war, is a kind of rationality[235] which is more influenced by 'familiarity'-explanations than by 'causality'-explanations. Calculation on the basis of 'familiarity' in relationships may well be 'stereotyped' and prejudiced. The 'expectation of war' as a contributory cause of war has already been suggested in sociological writings, and wiht good reason.[236].

In the second place it seems that the contributory causes which turn a situation into a conflict-situation are *infinite* in number. It may be submitted that even a subjective desire for conflict, the aggressive mood, is influenced by a great number of objective factors, some of

[232] In *The Nature of Conflict, op. cit. supra* n. 230 at 53. Cf. Jessie Bernard 'Parties and Issues in Conflict,' *Journal of Conflict Resolution*, Vol. I no. 2 (June 1957) 111ff.

[233] For earlier 'changes in the Foreign Policy mood' (including the American 'mood' about Russia) see: Gabriel A. Almond, *The American People and Foreign Policy*, New York. Harcourt, Brace & Co. (1950).

[234] T. Abel: 'The Element of Decisions in the Patterns of War,' *American Sociological Review* VI (1941) 853-859.

[235] 'rational,' exactly like 'justified', may mean that argument was heard and considered, or it may mean that there was good and wise (and ex *post facto* vindicated) judgment applied: two very different notions!

[236] Harold D. Lasswell, *World Politics and Personal Insecurity* (1935) Chapter III: The Balancing of Power: The Expectation of Violence, Reprinted in *A study of Power*, Glencoe, The Free Press (1950). Some sidelights on our 'Being in a Troublesome World': Hadley Cantril, *The Invasion from Mars*, Princeton University Press (1952).

which are not, as suggested by the 'positionalists,' incompatibility of goals but the coincidence of a convienient fighting opportunity. Often, of course, the opportunity, and particularly the chances of success, are merely assumed mentally, but often these mental assumptions at the back of political minds are more a contributory cause to the conflict than the 'incompatibility of goals.' These may be proclaimed as a 'casus belli' before and during a particular conflict and may in course of time disappear and be replaced by other socalled 'objective' reasons for a different conflict. It is submitted that the 'positional-sociological' approach to international conflict is justified in its criticism of the exaggerated 'tensions' ('war originates in the minds of men') approach but has itself three shortcoming:
a. it has not digested the distortions of rational argument and calculation, particularly when based on analysis by way of 'familiarity;[237]
b. it does not account for out-right persecution mania, or, in its mildest form, bickering, ill-will;[238]
c. it is unaware of the infinite complexity of inter-relationships leading to, or preventing and avoiding, conflict situations.

e. sociology: Population-Problems and Functionalism. It should be clear, that the sociological approach to International Relations comprises much more than two main streams of conflict theory. Sociology pays attention to population problems and, more than the geographical or economic approach, it pays attention to migration, its causes and the influence of migration on development,[239] to education, to cultural or racial minorities,[240] to communication, to cross-cultural contact.

There is a danger that these topics are becoming so fascinating to the theorist of International Relations, that they tend to dominate his

---

[237] An ample discussion of 'rationality' in conflict by Thomas C. Schelling, *The Strategy of Conflict*, Harvard University Press (1960) 16ff. and *passim*.
[238] Cf. R. Snyder's foreword in: M. Shubak, *Readings in Game Theory and Political Behaviour*, Garden City, Doubleday (1954).
[239] Cf. Donals R. Taft and Richard Robbins, *International Migrations*, New York, The Ronals Press (1955).
[240] Cf. Inis L. Claude Jr., *National Minorities*, Cambridge, Harvard University Press (1955).

approach one-sidedly. However, neglect of these topics impairs any previous approach mentioned.

We can not expect that Sociology will discover some kind of miracle-therapy for International Relations, as it may appear to have discovered for Industrial Relations, following the Hawthorne experiments and other work by Elton Mayo in particular. The restoration of human dignity in industrial relations, the emphasis on human problems besides questions of wages, working hours and physical working-conditions at the factory, and above all Mayo's success in demonstrating the employer's gain in improving these conditions, were corrections of the first order in mending some absurdities of a mis-applied Taylor-system and its mentality. The Mayo 'mentality' could have influenced programmes of international *personal* contact across frontiers, students' exchange and the like; all these cover a much smaller side of the great many issues involved in International Relations than their counterparts do in Industrial Relations.

The greatest contribution which may be expected from Sociology to International Relations is probably through the application of aspects of 'functionalism,' namely a further probing into the possibilities of establishing inter- or supra-national institutions with an economic or culturally limited task to perform. Some of the problems, touched upon in Ch. IV, I (g), will turn up again. The model of a functional division between authorities instead of the existing nationally divided authorities, attractive as it may appear, suffers from the same simplicity as the proposal that grown nations, with their grown web of loyalties, should simply just split up again. Harold Lasswell, among sociologists, has been quick to sense the difficulty inherent in each transfer of loyalty.[241]

Functionalism may be attempted on a less ambitious scale; yet the functional institutions to be set up must at least serve as a *brake* on strong national loyalties, otherwise these institutions would serve no useful purpose in the long run. An initial difficulty seems to be that the foundation of international institutions is largely a task for national governments, always reluctant to relinquish their basic justi-

---

[241] H. D. Lasswell op cit. *supra* n. 236, Ch. XI: 'In Quest of a Myth: The Problem of World Unity.'

fication (their appeal to national loyalties) in favour of international bodies. The real difficulty, however, is to conceive institutions and relationships capable of commanding loyalties competing with the existing national loyalties, institutions in a position to acquire meaning for individuals and groups beyond a vague symbolic appeal to universal peace and goodwill. This search for a utopian — yet relevant — re-organisation of loyalty-feelings might be, it is submitted, a foremost task for the sociological approach to International Relations. Such a task would, of necessity, divert some of the focus of attention away from the conflict-breeding aspects of international society towards those aspects which make for fellowship and joint effort. It is true enough that the conflict-situation for a group increases the sense of internal fellowship inside an involved group, but this does not yet necessarily mean that *only* the destructive conflict-situation vis-à-vis other human groups can produce these constructive human and social qualities.

CHAPTER V

NOTES ON METHODOLOGY

1. Lack of Disciplined Methodology

The submissions in the foregoing paragraphs seem to allow for a few remarks or suggestions in respect of the subject matter which must, of necessity, be covered by International Relations theory, and this will be attempted under four headings *infra* sub 2, (a, b, c and d).

The indication, however, of matters of interest for a developing theory does not solve ultimate methodological problems. If it were hoped that International Relations theory would, *at present*, evolve a clear cut method for research or for disciplined exposition, such hopes have not materialized and they do not, to me, seem realizable in the near future. On the contrary, it is better to say that, for the time being, the International Relations 'interest' (by which I mean something much less developed than a theory) leaves new methodological problems to the developing social sciences. A few of those problems may be deduced from the foregoing submissions. It is hoped that at least some of the remarks on history, political science and sociology were sufficiently suggestive in this respect. This is not to deny that, together with the growth of the International Relations *interest* a more suitable theory and more adequate methodological techniques may gradually evolve.

The position here defended, however, is, that so far all attempts to build a rigid and closed scientific discipline have been premature and may have the effect of stifling relevant research. The arguments for this view are, obviously, also (but not exclusively) connected with the suggestions as to the proper subject-matter of interest. That is to say: the wide variety of interests or topics which International Relations theory must serve or cover is by itself an indication (but not the only indication) of its un-disciplined state.

The growing and widening interest in the topics which International Relations covers is clear enough, but all the prompting motives are not, and closer scrutiny might well divulge concealed contradictions between the kinds of solution expected from the study of those topics (sub 3 *infra*). It would be surprising moreover if International Relations would lend itself to more desciplined study than do the Social Sciences in general. We should heed such warnings as not to 'believe that an empirically warranted theory, able to explain in terms of a single set of integrated assumptions the full variety of social phenomena, is likely to be achieved in the foreseeable future.'[242] Most social science systems are in danger of becoming too much 'single factor' or 'key cause' theories.[243] An additional and underrated danger for International Relations theory is that not enough questions (or not sufficiently cogent questions) have yet been asked. A theory can only develop its methodology when its principal questions have been discerned and properly arranged.

It is submitted once more that probably not enough questions have been discerned. One further suggestion in this respect is ventured: it may well be that close attention to *non*-international theory and research as well as to non-international occurrences may occasionally yield more profitable insights to International Relations theory than much pre-ordained analysis of international organizations, international conferences or international occurrences generally. Scrutiny and understanding of local events and of inter-group behaviour at events of seemingly mere 'national' importance may unexpectedly serve as an eye-opener.

2. Simultaneous Problematics

International Relations theory must probe in several directions simultaneously:

a. It needs at least some minimal appraisal of the external or environmental physical conditions under which human groups live and develop differentially (e.g. soil, water-supply, climate, transport facilities.)

[242] Ernest Nagel, *The Structure of Science*, London, Routledge & Kegan Paul (1961) in Ch. 13 'Methodological Problems of the Social Sciences' 448.
[243] Ernest Nagel: *ibid.* (note) 'They identify some one 'variable' — such as geographic environment, biological endowment, economic organization, or religious belief, to mention but a few — in terms of which the institutional arrangements and the development of societies are to be understood.'

b. The importance and relevance of the physical conditions and surroundings of people for International Relations theory vary with
their technical and social aspects (e.g. the ways and means of using
and modifying those conditions and the extent to which living conditions are related to surroundings).

c. Whilst potentially all the technical and social sciences have their
bearing on International Relations theory, in effect two highly dy-
namic aspects of central importance are likely to demand more attention than any other problem: the aspects of measuring *contiguity* (e.g.
how can one say how far any particular group extends; how far are
barriers somewhat artificially 'self-made' by the groups and how far
do they result from differentiated development over a period of time;
what institutions overcome existing barriers and what institutions increase their dividing force) as well as the aspect of gauging *continuity*
(e.g. how far can differentiated development of groups be seen as
continuous and not easily reversible; how far does it inescapably lead
to strife and conflict; how far does it — or does it not — escape political juridical and economic manipulation).

d. International Relations theory needs at least some minimal appraisal of the social institutions (e.g. governments, armies, law-courts,
educational systems) built by the groups, whether separately or to
some extent across the threshold of their respective barriers.

If these appraisals must all be discounted in International Relations
theory, the available methods of the social sciences must be exploited
to the utmost and a clear cut, new specific methodology is unlikely to
evolve, certainly not without severly limiting the viewpoints which
can be reached.

3. *Anxieties and Optimism Related to Methodology*

It is submitted that, to a substantial extent, growing interest in International Relations as a discipline was prompted by the quest for
greater security.

Escape from insecurity can be found, however, in several ways.
Some of these ways are incompatible with other wats, and if certain
theoretical indications would point to one kind of solution, a person

inwardly expecting a different solution will easily find fault with that solution and will find reasons for rejecting them.

In fact, it is submitted, adequate study of International Relations will — for some time to come — instill increased bewilderment and insecurity. This leads to a preference for research with a particular slant, where short-term results are promised or seem likely. Adequate general research, however, can not hold out any such promises of spectacular success in the near future and for that reason also seems less attractive.

To some extent it is possible to indicate what are the acceptable avenues of escape from prevailing insecurity and thus to understand better some methodological contradictions.

For present purposes avenues of escape from insecurity and acceptable ways of action may be classified as follows:

a. the way of the millennium, of 'perfect' International Relations (e.g. Peace through Law, World Government, An International Police Force, A Strong World Court, General and Complete Disarmament);

b. the way of peaceful diplomacy (e.g. good neighborly relations, regionalism, functionalism, strengthening International Organization, unselfish aid to underdeveloped countries);

c. the way of defense-diplomacy (e.g. economic and military alliances, defense-organization, aid to countries with visible or invisible strings attached);

d. the way of building military defense, which in the nature of things, must include the means of 'counter'-attack (e.g. increased and modernized armaments, spreading of industrial centres, upkeep of means of transport, training of the population).

The incompatibility of the extreme positions needs no elaboration. Nevertheless all the positions are taken — or furtively believed in — from time to time, and not only alternately but often side by side at the same moment.

If, for the sake of scientific exposition, a 'way of acting' or a 'system' can be distinctively — and somewhat abstractly — indicated, nevertheless in the fulness of life mixed systems and even contradictory-yet-simultaneous ways of acting will always occur. This makes the occurrence of 'true to type' systems, or 'typical representatives of a mode of thought' extremely rare. Notwithstanding this, even social scientists working with abstract models forget to keep constantly in mind that these models can not be more than an intellectual expedient; the very need to extract greater security from a chosen or expected avenue of analysis makes the representatives of one mode of thinking very intolerant of the adherents to a different approach.

Those who seek an international solution for some of the disasters of was soon believe that everything connected with war (training, discipline. preparedness even) is already disastrous in itself.

The advocates of the military approach, those aware of some implications of political 'brinkmanship'[244] (and there is much to learn from them for International Relations theory!) soon believe that those pleading for the 'good-neighborly' approach, are 'soft' and that those who plan for the millennium of perpetual peace are not only 'soft' but politically dangerous. Yet under present circumstances it can also be argued that, because of the cost of military defense which is wether in money, men, machinery or misery) wide beyond calculation, those who incline heavily towards military considerations are likewise politically dangerous. For that matter it is difficult to see how any political point of view would *not* involve great risks.

The high-pressure demands for 'better theory' in the discipline of International Relations are to no mean extent occasioned by the fact that serious research in this undisciplined branch gives to no one the security and the coherent results he would like to obtain. In the mass of contradictory trends and possibilities the counselors of despair and better-prepare-for-the-worst may seem able to bring more precise historical examples, more plausible arguments and intellectual support for an apparently realistic, even 'tough' policy. Nevertheless these tough realists usually hasten to add that they wish to speak only about 'short-run objectives'[245] and not about any hopelessness in general.

It is not amazing that methodological differences in approach reflect different fundamental philosophical approaches and that differ-

[244] Thomas C. Schelling, *op. cit. supra* n. 237 at 199ff.
[245] Quince Wright, *op. cit. supra* n. 12 at 7ff remarks that the pursuit of long run policies may often be deflected by short run necessities.

ences in theoretical analysis of social phenomena are bound up with deep-seated or half-hidden psychological expectations. 'Toughness' in International Relations theory, however, is not the same as courage, it may even betray a lack of courage to admit that this theory is a very unfinished affair. Theoreticians who use peaceful models on the other hand, do not necessarily lack courage, unless they actually fail to admit the imperfections of such models.

As a last submission in this paper, therefore, I would argue for the scientific legitimacy of using, in International Relations theory, abstract models, 'ideal types', envisaging, with all due prudence. a much more peaceful international society than in which we actually live.

CHAPTER VI

POSTSCRIPT

1. The Stream of Thought in Perspective

This study, which appeared in 1963, was sold out in 1968. Early in 1970 the publishers expressed their desire to have a new edition prepared. This undertaking, which necessitates considerable re-thinking and an extensive new elaboration of text and notes, is still in the planning stage. The present intermediate solution — an unaltered re-edition with a postscript — signifies, naturally, that I still endorse most of the original text. In particular there are good grounds to repeat again and again the warnings against a false belief in masterkeys to a new international relations theory.

Assuming, of course, that these continuous warnings will be heeded, the original reasons to defend the final conclusion of the study are still valid, namely, the legitimacy of using abstract models, 'ideal types', envisaging a much more peaceful international society than the one in which we live or have been living for the past decade.

The enormous expansion of what has come to be known as 'Peace Research' seems to do just that and to signify the development of international relations research with the aid of a more peaceful conceptualization of the future both as an august hope and a constant challenge. Certainly, much of what has been published under the rather indiscriminate cover of 'peace research' (or within the volumes of a new Journal of Peace Research appearing since 1964) gives relevant theoretical conjectures and insights in the study of international relations. Nevertheless the designation of all these studies as 'Peace Research' does not thereby revolutionize pre-existing theory. Practically every word of what was written in Chapter III, Section 6 a-c (pp.57-59) above, under Pacifism, is applicable to such publications. I must add however, that the very term 'peace research' is unfortunate[1] in that it may contribute to the defeat of its own objectives: it

[1] The author refers to his former objections in *Research for Peace* (note 12 *supra*) and most recently in *A Prologue to Peace Research*, Jerusalem, Israel Universities Press; Amsterdam, North Holland Publishing (1071).

threatens to give rise to false illusions; it tends to call for anodyne rather than for painstaking analysis, and it often results in a disproportionate emphasis on conflict situations and their attempted resolution. The term has apparently left far too little scope for philosophical reflection, or at least obscured the fact that the essence of peace research is but the continuation of the concern with society in classical philosophy.

The subject of philosophical perspective leads to the debates, often in the form of disconnected monologues, which were carried on at te Karlovy Vary Meetings (1969) of the International Peace Research Association, dedicated to 'the nature and philosophy of peace research'. A conspicuous misjudgment in these debates (displayed in particular, but not exclusively, by the revolutionary spokesmen who bore the banner of the New Left) was that of seeing peace research as a new scientific venture. This fitted in with the New Left vision of peace research as a modern tool for exploiters, developed by social scientists solely for the benefit of the 'wicked' establishment. The Proceedings show that this rather remarkable accusation was made and, at least to the satisfaction of those of the participants who were sufficiently unbiassed, refuted.[2] However, more attention should have been paid to the fact that peace research is not as new an enterprise as the least reasonable amongst peace researchers tend to assume: a more thorough study of classical philosophers will reveal that many of their contributions must also be justifiably classed as peace research.

Wilst this Postscript must, of course, take into account the changed slant that has taken place in the study of international relations, resulting from this upsurge of peace research, the limitations of this recent trend should not be forgotten.

We may as well remember that up-dating always runs the risk of devoting too much attention to the new and the recent, sometimes entirely by virtue of their novelty. In updating, anything that is not quite fresh tends to be dismissed as obsolete. Thus one overlooks what preceded or even evoked the latest publications. In no case are we entitled to say that the latest survey is necessarily the best or the most

---

[2] *Proceedings of the Third IPRA General Conference* (Karlovy Vary, 1969), Vol. 1, Assen, Van Gorcum (1970)

competently executed one, just because it happens to be the most up-to-date or the most exhaustive in scope.

Every up-dating, other than a compilation of mechanical indexes. tends to be highly selective. Moreover, during the last decade a good many publications in our field were themselves compilations or collective surveys of views propounded in the past. In this connection I must repeat that the original motive for this book was not, as the representative of any particular school, to join in, let alone settle, the debate as to what is proper 'theory' for the field. Nor was it my intention to render a comprehensive account of the theories which can — or could — be said to exist. It is true, however, that the attempts at putting a definitive international relations theory on the map or at registering prevalent theoretical doctrine were what prompted my analysis. It was meant as an over-all, critical appraisal of, and a further provocative stimulant towards the early 'theory'-debate.[3] I then thought, and think still, that none of the newly discovered building tools useful for a developing international relations theory make earlier classical approaches superfluous. Modern analysis is always somehow related to pre-existing tools of analysis and understanding. It is only with the *useful* new tools that I have been dealing and I am not at all insensitive to such sharpened sociological methods as quantitative measurement, factor analysis, or indicators, nor to any of the concepts and constructs discussed hereafter (Sections 2-9). I trust however, that I am not being unfair in proposing that their usefulness still lies well within the traditional development of classical philosophy and political thought, beginning with that of the Greeks, through that of such early masters of European thought as Machiavelli and Bacon. White's recent brilliant analysis of the political philosophy of Francis Bacon, with due reference to the peaceful model in his *New Atlantis*[4], can be cited as surprising evidence of the present interest in and validity of writings published more than three centuries ago, which, in turn, contained so many allusions to even older wisdom. It

---

[3] This was, as already gratefully acknowledged, first suggested by Bernard H. M. Vlekke (now deceased), but to no mean extent Bert V.A. Röling, Julius Stone and others sustained me and helped me on the way to make such a contribution.
[4] Howard B. White, *Peace among the Willows*, the Hague, Martinus Nijhoff (1968).

also proves that in political theory the breach with former streams of thought is — and perhaps will remain — less radical than in the natural and technical sciences.

2. Peace Research

An impressive, fairly comprehensive (and comparatively short — at about 300 pages) report on recent developments, particularly in the United States, of studies related to the causes of war, begins its foreword with two very challenging statements:

> This book documents a revolution in our thinking. War and peace have, in the last decade, become respectable research topics for a significant number of social and behavioral scientists of varying disciplinary backgrounds who look at them as empirical phenomena to be explained. For the first time in history, we can speak of a 'Peace Research Movement', characterized by rigorous empirical inquiry into the nature and origins of violence in international conflict.[5]

The authors give due credit to substantial prior literature and they admit that the strategic, deterrence and conflict research programs inaugurated in the late 1950's 'received considerable intellectual stimulation from the older field of international politics, which had broken out of its historical mold' and which, the authors hopefully believe, was commencing on 'the long road to a general theory of international relations.'[6] The authors also mention the impossibility of attributing the origin of wars to any unique cause. They are careful about defining 'good' theory and formulate very strict criteria for a 'proper' case method, and for permissible variables in empirical research. They go on to analyse recent studies of the causes of war, which they regard as an essential advance of peace research and hence also of the study of international relations. The high standard of this survey and the excellence of the considerable research material referred to, make it tempting to consider whether this recent respecta-

---

[5] Dean G. Pruitt and Richard C. Snyder, *Theory and Research on the Causes of War*, Englewood Cliffs, Prentice-Hall, (1969), p. IX.
[6] *Id.*, p. X.

bility of peace research has essentially changed international relations theory.

For this purpose it is well to remember that peace research is by no means a clearly defined discipline — its field of research is not even remotely definable.[7] To say the least, peace research and international relations theory originated in the same set of problems. As Röling so convincingly demonstrated in his foreword to the present study, the two are chapters of one another. One could, I think. expand this and argue that peace research and international relations theory are almost identical. Admittedly, peace researchers are committed to the study of international relations with a certain slant towards and stress upon the remedial objectives of their study. But students of international relations can never close their eyes completely to remedial objectives. I can but repeat my earlier submission in Chapter V, 3 (p.94) that 'to a substantial extent, growing interest in International Relations as a discipline was prompted by the quest for greater security.'

The requirement to relate war an peace between nations to war and peace between classes, races, and religious affiliations may, superficially, seem one of peace research rather than one of the study of international relations; the neglect resulting from such a superficial apodictive attitude would greatly impoverish international relations theory. Tensions between minorities or sub-groups easily spill over into tensions between nations. All the tools of analysis, such as strategy, simulation, development (section 3 - 9 below) in peace research invariably appear as added dimensions in the study of international relations. It is well nigh impossible to arbitrarily allocate such tools to one field of endeavour rather than the other.

In brief — peace research has widened the dimensions of international relations theory, but has not changed its nature, not made it more scientific, and not delimited its field in any precise way.

To say, appreciatively, that peace research has widened the dimensions of international relations theory is not merely a matter of the past tense. Peace research itself must, and it is hoped will, expand into still wider fields of inquiry beyond those of the empirical causes

---

[7] Julius Stone, *Research for Advancement of Peace,* Jerusalem, Truman Centre (1968). Charles Boasson, *op. cit.* (1971) note [1] *supra.*

of war, or the theoretical conditions of peace. Apart from the required philosophical expansion at the highest level, alluded to before, there are important implications, at a more elementary, in particular educational, level. This may eventually include the education of politicians towards better reading, understanding and using the means of communication before pent-up frustrations turn these into destructive communication by violent protest. Such studies as are now in progress at the Groningen Polemological Institute, with the cooperation of teachers at primary and secondary schools, to probe the possibilities of change and the growth of international awareness, may promote a further widening of our conceptional horizon as well as a change in some ethnocentric tenets of the prevailing educational value system.

3. Strategic Thinking

Reflection on the elements of strategy enlightens us further on the near-identity and almost total overlap of peace research on the one hand and international relations theory on the other.

Strategic thinking includes strategies for a peaceful solution as much as strategies in violent conflict; cooperation for the achievement of a common purpose as much as the elimination of competition or opposition. In this field game theory has developed useful cooperative strategy models and calculations on how a basic cooperative attitude is likely to be most conducive to the attainment of objectives even when the attitude of the other parties involved is uncertain and when an anti-cooperative relapse is always likely.[8]

A common way of thinking treats the conduct of international bargaining and the taking of positions *as if* the threats of war could be balanced; the threat of war has always been considered quite a weighty component in one's bargaining position as well as an alterna-

---

[8] The 'gaming section' in the *Journal of Conflict Resolution* dealt with this problem many times, usually with elaborations of the Prisoner's Dilemma game. *E.g.* V. Edwin Bixenstine, Clifford A. Levitt and Kellogg V. Wilson, 'Collaboration among six persons in a Prisoners Dilemma game'. Vol. X, 488 - 496.
Robert L. Swinth, 'The establishment of the trust relationship', Vol. XI, 335 - 344.
Donnel Wallace and Paul Rothaus, 'Communication, group loyalty and trust in the PD game', Vol XIII, 370 - 380. A very 'sportive' article is further: Günther Lüschen, 'Cooperation, association and contest', Vol. XIV 21 - 34.

tive means of achieving results. The implied assumption made in this type of peace research is that these traditional actions of the Nation-State cannot be expected to undergo fundamental change. (However understandable this assumption may be, it requires critical analysis, but this is not the issue here.) A valuable example is Boulding's theoretical approach to 'conflict and defense'.[9] Although Boulding pays due attention to non-international conflicts (e.g., economic, industrial, ideological, and ethical), his main stress is on international conflict, which is characterized by 'a dramatic alternation' of two contrasted forms of conflict, namely, diplomacy (a conflict situation where peace still exists, but is threatened) and war.[10]

This means, obviously. that for a proper understanding of a general theory of conflict and defense — whether set up as peace research, as strategy research, or as the study of war — it is always incumbent on the researcher to master a general theory of international politics at the same time. It is therefore not accidental that Boulding appreciates how well Clausewitz understood 'both the unity of the system of diplomacy and war and of its two sharply contrasted patterns,' and this in spite of many misconceptions about Clausewitz's pioneering studies.[11]

When discussing one of his central defense concepts — the forces that determine the loss-of-strength gradient (L.S.G.) of a nation — Boulding refers by clear implication to the analysis of international

---

[9] Kenneth E. Boulding, *Conflict and Defense* — A General Theory, New York, Harper & Row, (1962; Harper Torchbook Edition 1963).

[10] *Id.*, p. 227 of Torchbook edition.

[11] *Id.*, p. 249.

As to a new interest in Von Clausewitz, see:

A French complete edition (1955) by Editions de Minuit and excerpts of that translation by Denise Naville in a pocketbook edition, selected, introduced and commented upon by Pierre Naville: Carl von Clausewitz, *de la guerre* Paris, Editions de Minuit (1955 with postscript 1965).

New English editions: New York, Barnes & Noble (1956); London, translation by Col. J. J. Graham, edited by Col. F. N. Maude (1962).

Further: Roger Ashley Leonard, *A Short Guide to Clausewitz on War*, London, Weidenfeld and Nicolson (1967).

Michael Howard, 'War as an instrument of policy', chapter 10 in Herbert Butterfield and Martin Wight (eds.) *Diplomatic Investigations*, London, Allen & Unwin (1966) pp. 193 - 200.

relations *in their totality*. This L.S.G. is 'the degree to which [a nations'] military and political power diminishes as we move a unit distance away from its home base' — and these forces 'depend on a host
of geographical, psychological, and organizational factors.'[12]

It is worthwhile to compare this necessary and correct referral in a
theoretical work with its frequent neglect in historical or empirical
analyses of specific conflict situations.[13]

Indeed the intertwined relationships between the geographical, the
economical, the political, and the psychological, and the unstable pre-
ponderance of each factor in turn, makes the theoretical study of international relations so difficult and uncertain and contemporary or
historical descriptions thereof often so misleading.

Whilst peace research tends to fuse with international relations theory, strategy does not. The subject of strategic thinking is on the one
hand much narrower than either theory of peace or that of international relations. One of the reasons is that strategy, by definition,
concentrates on conflict situations and neither peace research nor international relations theory should. Not even politics, as argued before, are dominated by conflict to that extent . It is the preoccupation
with international conflict which makes the strategic theories of Beaufre so narrow, inspite of his flowery expression 'la stratégie totale'
and his equation of strategy and modern politics. Although he accuses
others of pseudo-clausewitzian aberrations, it remains doubtful
whether he has thought through the implications of Clausewitz to the
end.[14]

---

[12] Boulding, *op. cit.* note [9], Appendix to Chapter 12, pp. 245 - 247.

[13] We can mention a work like Evan Luard, *Conflict and Peace in the Modern International System,* Boston, Little, Brown and Co., (1968); this 'attempts to provide
a general introduction to international relations, based on a purely emprirical approach to the subject' (Preface, p. V) and thus explicitly takes this near identity between strategy analysis and international relations study as self understood, but
does not bring it out as strikingly as does Boulding nor, perhaps, as fully.

[14] What I wrote in 1963 (sub IV, 2, *e supra*, pp. 77 - 78) has found confirmation in
the discussion between Professors Banfield and Vernon Vandyke, in particular
where the latter finally accepted valuable non-conflict aspects of political science.
Vernon Vandyke, 'The optimum scope of political science' in J. C. Charlesworth
(ed), *A Design for Political Science,* Philadelphia, American Academy of Political
Social Science (1966).

On the other hand, however, strategy is much wider than international relations theory, because it deals with the reaching of goals, any goals, while overcoming opposition. Such goals may be the winning of a football competition, or of a municipal election, and strategic insights in these pursuits may, but need not be related to any insights in politics or international relations. In this sense strategy is rather on a par with planning and development and, in some respects covered by — or covers — communication theory.

International conflicts may be resolved by different strategies. Military strategy is one: military success (or the mere possibility of military success) can occasionally resolve a conflict. This, of course, is not always uppermost in the minds of those who engage — with the intentions of a peace researcher or peace maker — in 'conflict resolution' and when they occasionally neglect this factor altogether, their proposals become unhelpful.

As against these lofty peace strategists there are down-to-earth strategists, who hope to provide their defense ministries with some theoretical basis to be used as guidelines. This is, of course, a time-honoured pursuit, and such strategists are, and always have been in danger of finding their theories outdated by the technical innovations of their own comtemporaries (to say nothing of those of the following generations). They are also in danger of being overconcerned with short-range analysis of immediate crises. Notwithstanding this, even such short-term strategic considerations deserve attention; these may have been somewhat neglected in this study,[15] and it is impossible to say which amongst the spate of contemporaneous strategic studies

Compare my *A Prologue to Peace to Peace Research, op. cit.* note [1] *supra.* And note [16] *infra.*

[15] Strategic political polemics having at the same time a scientific quality are e.g.: Bernard Brodie, *Strategy in the Missile Age*, Princeton U.P. (1957, new Princeton Paperback edition 1965 and Henry A. Kissinger, *Nuclear Weapons and Foreign Policy*, New York, Harper & Bros (1957; abridged Doubleday Anchor Books Edition 1958).

[16] Apart from Boulding, *op. cit.* note [9] *supra*, one could refer to two books, much publicised at the time, by General Beaufre, *Introduction à la stratégie* and *Dissuasion et Stratégie*, Paris, Armand Colin (1963 and 1964).

A comprehensive study is Y. Harkabi, *Nuclear War and Nuclear Peace*, Jerusalem, Israel Program for Scientific Translations (1966).

of disarmament of 'arms-control' is worthless, or harmful, unless strategic considerations of *all* kinds are taken into account.

The special joint issue (September/October 1963) of the *Journal of Conflict Resolution* and the *Journal of Arms Control* provides the required juxtaposition of factors concerned.[17] The suggestion by Abt, in his article 'Arms Control and Strategy', in that issue, namely — that disarmament conferences may serve the purpose of a step-up in armament strategy, has become almost the central thesis of Spanier and Nogee in their perceptive study.[18]

It is still too early at the moment of writing to say what will be the final results of the SALT (Strategic Arms Limitations Talks) consultations at present in progress, nor is it possible to predict whether these consultations will develop in something permanent. This would, however limited in scope, mean a certain institutional success. Röling has justly remarked in his analysis of SALT written at the request of and in cooperation with the Dutch Interchurch Peace Council, during 1970, that the civil populations are being made into hostages for a possible limitation of nuclear arms, if the talks will be successful.

Also to be considered are the strategic and outright warlike aims pursued by some movements advocating 'non-violenec' or 'passive resistance'. On the one hand, these movements might claim to promote 'peaceful change' (or peaceful irredentism, perhaps), but on the other hand this is a method of inaugurating a struggling sequel to a defeat in battle.[19] The fact that the resisters are often morally superior to the authorities resisted does not mean that such nonviolent means of protest and revolt are morally justified *per se,* or that the lines between terrorist attacks (be they directed against civilian or military targets)

---

[17] J. David Singer (ed.), 'Weapons Management in World Politics,' *The Journal of Conflict Resolution,* Vol. II, no. 5 (or *Journal of Arms Control,* Vol. I, no. 4).
[18] Clark C. Abt, 'Disarmament as a Strategy', *id.* pp. 293 - 308 (or 387 - 402).
John W. Spanier and Joseph L. Nogee, *The Politics of Disarmament,* A Study in Soviet — American Gamesmanship, New York, Praeger (1962).
[19] A good general review is given in William Robert Miller, *Non-violence,* A Christian Interpretation, New York, Shocken Books (1966). Compare my criticism of blind acceptance of Gandhi's 'satyagraha' in *A Prologue to Peace Research, op. cit,* note [1] *supra.*

and true non-violent resistance can always be drawn.[20] Often the sympathies of the observer colour the ultimate description of the behaviour to such extent, that dastardly criminal attacks on innocent victims are exalted as moral heroism.

It is in any case true that both underground and open resistance, whether violent or not, are factors to be considered in any war-strategy, just as war-strategy has to be considered in the study of international relations.[21]

4. International Communications

When discussing Diplomacy and Information in chapter II, 2.b. (pp.28,29) I limited myself to the *gathering* of information. I did not deal so much with other aspects of information and communications theory which have become increasingly central to the evaluation of international situations. Not only have the means of obtaining and analysing information — even of a semi-secret nature — vastly increased; diplomats or the official press are often expected to 'leak' information of a quasi-confidential nature, 'messages' as to how a country is able and likely to act under certain circumstances.

The possibilities in this sphere have been considerably broadened by modern means of mass-communication such as radio, which, more than the printed word, can reach audiences across political borders and independently of the audience's own national news sources.

---

[20] It is not always possible to draw sharp lines between civil disobedience and guerilla warfare, although separate strategies have evolved for each. Compare Miller, *Non-violence, op. cit.* (previous note) with Robert Taber, *The War of the Flea,* London, Paladin Paperback (1970, after the American edition of 1965).

[21] This, of course, has long been understood. An early modernized condensation of this insight is found in Klaus Knorr, *The War Potential of Nations,* Princeton, U.P. (1956).

A comprehensive discussion of such recent concepts as 'deterrence', 'balance of terror', 'brinkmanship,' 'communication,' 'limited war,' 'overkill' and others in Thomas C. Schelling *Arms and Influence,* New haven, Yale U.P. (1966). For official and semi-official government attitudes of those days, including those of the USSR, see John Erickson (ed.) *The Military-Technical Revolution,* London, Pall Mall Press (1966)

One of the first to identify this use of the means of communication as an element in the game of brinkmanship was the sensitive French journalist Geneviève Tabouis who, in the first month of 1938, wrote these far-seeing words in respect of purposely publicized speeches:

> Perhaps war does not pay, but blackmail, based on the threat of war, certainly did.

and:

> Of course, Italy and Germany are bluffing. The danger is, however, that sooner or later the successes scored by Rome and Berlin as a result of their blackmailing methods will encourage one or other of the dictators, caught in his own trap, to gamble for the mastery of Europe by means of a stupendous war, which incidentally, would save him from his serious internal troubles.[22]

Thus, at one and the same time, the author indicated this overspill of internal communications into the reality of international relations, and the interaction between all kinds of communication.

This factor has since been analyzed more closely, often under the express heading of 'international political communications'. Not everything which is leaked to the news media is willingly given to them; at least as frequently it is diligently ferreted out and even harmfully overplayed. The exclamation of Robert Manning (the editor of the *Atlantic Monthly*) can be well understood, when he said: 'Freedom of the Press is too important a right to be left only to the publishers. editors, broadcasters and reporters.'[23]

---

[22] Geneviève Tabouis, *Blackmail or War*, Harmondsworth, Penguin Books (1938) pp. 8, 9.
[23] See e.g. W. Phillips Davison, *International Political Communication*, New York, Praeger (1965).
Other aspects of 'policy, press and public opinion in Asian-American relations' were analysed by John Hohenberg, *Between Two Worlds*, New York, Praeger (1967).
Throughout Arthur S. Hoffman (ed.) *International Communication and the New Diplomacy* Indiana U.P. (1968) pertinent consideration to this development is given: in particular Bryant Wedge, 'Communication Analysis and Comprehensive Diplomacy,' pp' 24 - 47, Lloyd A. Free, 'Public Opinion Research' pp. 48 - 63; Daniel Lerner, 'Pshychology and Psychological Operations' pp. 124 - 136; Robert Manning, 'International News Media' pp. 147 - 167; the quotation is from p. 149.

Very recently Robert Jervis made a helpful distinction between 'signals' and 'indices', describing ways and means to influence the 'images' which prevail in the dialogue between nations.[24] Often a communication contributes less to make an image than does the influence of a prior stereotype on the reception of a certain communication. The press adapts itself to the prevailing prejudices. Even the more informed receivers of any news item evaluate it according to their preconceived ideas. Thus, news from certain sources, when considered as originating from 'the enemy', are for that reason more suspect, more dangerous, or more subject to scrutiny than the same news would be if thought to emanate from friendly or neutral sources.[25]

Senders of messages may be so caught up in their own web of preconceptions that they miscalculate the effect their own messages have on their receivers, or even err in assuming blithely that their message has *got through,* beyond the first barrier. The latter problem was completely overlooked in the early stages of so-called 'technical aid' programs and it is hardly ten years since it has begun to be better understood. We have seen this problem already raised in ongoing peace research and we will meet it again in the critical development reports referred to later.[26]

5. Quantitative International Politics

It is only with a refinement in the evaluation of communications, emitted and received, that some hesitant insights of quantitative measurement could be achieved. Quantification is, in effect, a specifically

[24] Robert Jervis, *The Logic of Images in International Relations*, Princeton, U.P. (1970).
[25] Very useful theoretical and empirical studies on many aspects of this problem are found in David J. Finlay, Ole R. Holsti and Richard R. Fagen, *Enemies in Politics*, Chicago, Rand McNally and Co. (1967).
[26] Pioneering studies were submitted to the Conference on Communication and Political Development held on September 11-14, 1961, at Gould House, Dobbs Ferry, New York. See: Lucien W. Pye, (ed), *Communications and Political Development*, Princeton U.P. (1963).
For an informative later study see:
Daniel Lerner and Wilbur Schramm, *Communication and Change in the Developing Countries*, Honolulu, East-West Center Press (1967).
See also notes [49] and [50] *infra.*

defined manner of communicating. It often *seems* more precise than it really is and warnings are required on all fronts in this respect.

In the first place, neither scales nor statistics nor the discovery of trends necessarily mean or imply true quantification. We must distinguish between the restricted use of selected comparative units (which are only rough indicators on minor aspects of the total situation) and a complete and exactly measured comparison of all relevant quantities. For example, we can make an exact comparison between the body temperatures and pulse rates of one person at different times of the day, or between the temperatures and pulse rates of different persons at a given moment. Complete and exact quantification exists here, but such information is for a physician restricted and does not suffice to diagnose a person's state of health or compare the relative health of individuals in a group. Nevertheless, curves, or comparative statistics can be drawn up, and insights can be gained from these very limited exact data, and these in turn can be extrapolated into much more general (albeit less accurate) statements.[27]

In the second place. there are very few topics in international relations where data can be so assessed as to enable the scholarly community to agree on comparable statistics, data, or developments. True, results of public-opinion polls and estimates of gross national output can be rendered in figures, but — in order to be significant — data collection must be continuous, and even well-documented trends can be reversed by unforeseen developments or bij events too ambivalent to have been taken into account. Such pioneering efforts as those of Bruce M. Russett *e.a.* to summarize 'indicators'[28] and those of Karl

---

[27] A warning, very much akin to my submission in the text, not to equate measurement, quantification and mathematization as being interchangeable in: Robert T. Golembiewski, William A. Welsh and William J. Crotty, *A Methodological Primer for Political Scientists,* Chicago, Rand McNally & Co (1969) at p. 439, This warning implies criticism of the too easily presumed 'order' in scientific progress, mentioned by these authors earlier (p. 32): 'empirical regularities — quantification — mathematization'. No scientific progress is as simple as that.

[28] Bruce M. Russet and Hayward R. Alker Jr., Karl W. Deutsch, Harold D. Lasswell, *World Handbook of Political and Social Indicators,* Yale U.P. (1964).

Richard L. Merrit and Stein Rokkan (eds.) *Comparing Nations, The Use of Quantitative Data in Cross National Research,* Yale U.P. (1965).

Deutsch *e.a.* to construe communications as a quantifiable quality, need constant repetition.[29]

Finally, major reservations must be expressed with regard to the more ambitious attempts at quantifying behaviour and using the results for predictive purposes. David J. Singer *e.a.*,[30] who recently published a most thorough survey of what methods have been introduced as quantitative international politics, explain in their methodological clarifications that there is, as yet, no more than an early and rough theoretical basis to work upon. No immediate practical results must be expected.[31]

Quantification and mathematical manipulation are aids to theory, and certainly not theory *per se*. Even the most sophisticated aid to theory may be misleading when the theory itself cannot direct or digest the means at its disposal. As Singer has put it, these (in a way, mechanical) aids 'need to flow from a coherent and developing theoretical framework.[32] Deficient data are often the cause of theoretical shortcomings in international relations theory: quantifiers who know to select, handle and evaluate data, are therefore entitled to a hearing. Nevertheless, it is submitted that data-processing — precisely those aids to theory where quantification is most important — always needs further guidance which quantification *by itself* cannot supply, namely, guidance as to the ranking (possibly in a fluctuating order

---

[29] Karl W. Deutsch, *op. cit.* note 56, *supra;*
Karl W. Deutsch and Lewis J. Edinger, *op. cit.* note 21 *supra;*
Later work of those two authors (with Ray C. Macridis, Richard L. Merrit): *France, Germany and the Western Alliance*, New York, Charles Scribner & Sons (1967) rightly stresses some 'latent' attitudes (*id.* 186, 187).

[30] J. David Singer (ed) *Quantitative International Politics*, New York, The Free Press (1968).

[31] One should admit, with Arthur Lee Burns, *Of Powers and their Politics, A Critique of Theoretical Approaches*, Englewood Cliffs, Prentice Hall (1968) that 'it is no longer a plausible criticism that political scientists quantifying world affairs merely reproduce in statistical disguise what everyone knows already'. Surprises are indeed possible, although in the instance quoted (Arab and Latin American voting for U.N. supranationalism *correlated* with percentage of U.S., French or U.K. trade, pp. 174 - 181) the surprise correlates somewhat with lack of inside ànd overall knowledge.

[32] J. David Singer, *op. cit.* note [30] *supra* p. 2.

according to various sets of circumstances) of the relevance of available data.

Quantitative international politics remain meaningless without adequate meta-quantitative international relations theory.

6. Simulation in International Relations

If quantification is an aid in theory-formation and understanding, simulation originated as an aid in learning processes and as a supplementary tool in teaching and research. Simulation was quite widely used even before 1963. but it was with the publication, in that year, of the major survey of the implications and perspectives of this technology,[33] that simulation came into its own among the community of scholars and was vigorously embraced by them.

Wide-scale adaptations and imitations of the technique followed, some of them lacking the sophistication and theoretical alertness of the original example. This may have resulted partly from the idea that the use of computers and other laboratory mechanics[34] were the supplementary tools, and that simulation constituted already *the* theory. A better reading of what the original authors, Guetzkow and others, had to say would have prevented this error, since in their foreword they stated that 'no one [at Northwestern, where the program was developed] holds the belief that the inter-nation simulation is

[33] The most exemplary exposition, even now, still seems this fascinating book: Harold Guetzkow, Chadwick F. Alger, Richard A. Brody, Robert C. Naeland and Richard C. Snyder, *Simulation in International Relations: Development for Research and Teaching*. Englewood Cliffs, Prentice Hall (1963).
The present author gratefully acknowledges a most stimulating letter he received from Professor Guetzkow soon after the first publication of these *Approaches*, which letter also drew attention to the fruitful simulation approach.
Admittedly the general overview of internation simulation, given by Guetzkow in chapter two of the above book, had appeared already in the July, 1959, issue of *Behavioral Science*.

[34]. Pictures and examples abound throughout the book by Guetzkow e.a. (id. *passim*).
Compare also: Ithiel de Sola Pool and Allan Kessler, 'The Kaiser, the Tsar and the Computer: Information Processing in a Crisis'. Vol. 8 (May 1965), *The American Behavioral Scientist* 31 - 38 (reprinted in Naomi Rosenbaum (ed.) *Readings on the International Political System*, Englewood Cliffs, Prentice Hall (1970) pp. 91 - 111.

more than a supplemental tool to our more traditional ways of building theory about international affairs.'

Remarkable parallels were discovered between the behaviour of actors in the simulation process and that of participants on the real scene, and some came to believe that valid conclusions could be drawn from the laboratory experiments. Richard C. Snyder has warned, however, that 'simple laboratory operations observed by a neophyte are likely to be interpreted literally, a circumstance that obscures the complicated creation of analysis.'[25] This remark can, of course, be extended to historical analysis; in more ways than one, the predictive powers of simulated events are similar to those of the study of history, not only for the reason that simulations are modelled on historical examples. Simulation, exactly like history, is for International Relations Theory 'suggestive, but no more' (see Chapter III, 4.d.p.49 above), and this for reasons indicated by the originators of this useful tool for study and research.

7. Animal Behaviour

The observation of human behaviour, whether in history or in simulations thereof, invites a comparison with the behaviour of animals.

The danger is, of course, that observers of the animal kingdom can turn into immature philosophers jumping to ungrounded — and, indeed, totally invalid — conclusions regarding the human race. In the words of Elton B. McNeil: 'discoveries with animals can be applied to man or another society of animals only through reasoning by analogy. Work on one species can serve as model only for the formulation of *hypotheses* about other species.'[36] John H. Herz also took issue, and rightly so, with biologists who categorically assume immutable instincts and other behavioural patterns on the basis of some-

---

[35] Richard C. Snyder, 'Some Perspectives on the Use of Experimental Techniques in the Study of International Relations' in Guetzkow *et al., op. cit,* note [33] *supra,* pp. 1 - 23 at p. 5.
[36] Elton B. McNeil 'The Nature of Aggression' in: Elton B. McNeil (ed.), *The Nature of Human Conflict,* Englewood Cliffs. Prentice Hall (1965) pp. 14 - 41 at p. 5.

times slender evidence.[37] It is somewhat surprising, however, to find that Herz considers Robert Ardrey to be a mere 'popularizer' in the wake of Lorenz. Without underrating the importance of Lorenz as an observer of wild life, and as a fascinating author, part of his book *On Agression*, especially its concluding chapter, is indeed a crude popularization.[38] In comparison, Ardey's *The Territorial Imperative* seems thoughtful throughout; moreover, it provides the reader with a mine of valuable references, about some of which Ardrey justifyably waxes lyrical.[39]

As a basic hypothesis and possible explanation for certain defensive (but warlike) attitudes, the primitive attachment to territory deserves close attention. What should be added, however, apart from all the essential differences between animals and human beings, is that the territorial 'imperative' is not even all that imperative in the animal kingdom itself. There is the riddle of animal migration. not unconnected with a return to identical locations, but nevertheless opening up altogether different vista.[40] There is, above all, the riddle (not often stressed) of animal sociability. The outstanding example — and one from which the human race could benefit by humble learning — is the dolphin, the most cheerful and helpful of living creatures. If one argues that such absolute absence of aggressive attitudes as the dolphin displays[41] is beyond human attainment, it does not dispose of

---

[37] John H. Herz, 'The Territorial State Revisited,' II (1968) *Polity* 12 - 34, reprinted as chapter 8 in James N. Rosenau (ed.), *International Politics and Foreign Policy*, New York, The Free Press (1969) pp. 76 - 89.
[38] Konrad Lorenz, *Das sogenannte Böse (Zur Naturgeschichte des Aggression)*, Vienna, Borotha-Schoeler (1963).
The title itself is biassed; a thorough criticism of this approach in: Rolf Denker, *Aufklärung über Aggression*, Stuttgart, Kohlhammer (1966).
[39] Robert Ardrey, *The Territorial Imperative*, London, Collins (1967; Fontana Library edition 1969).
[40] For a general survey see: Otto von Frisch, *Animal Migration*, London, Collins (1969).
[41] Robert Stenuit, *The Dolphin, Cousin to Man*, London, Dent & Sons 1968.
Stenuit reports (p. 2) 'but never, absolutely never, has a dolphin or a porpoise attacked a man, even in legitimate defense, with a harpoon in its side or when, with electrodes in its skull it has been massacred in the name of science'.

the example as a moral guidepost, superior to anything else in our natural or cultural environment.[42]

Another point that needs further elucidation is the intimate connection between the social and historical aspects of fear in the human context, which leads to the entrenchment of aggressive-defensive reaction patterns and to a consequent automatic repetition of performances established by previous similar events. Such a memorized reaction pattern can never be compared with an animal's primitive instinctive reaction, in spite of some evident similarity. The recent symposium on scientific research for advancement of peace, held in Brussels, rightly stressed again the social aspects of fear and anxiety.[43] Proper understanding in this field cannot be based on animal psychology alone.

8. Population and Ecology

The Malthusian aspect of International Relations is still very much with us (see above, chapter III.3.d.pp.41, 42) though new dimensions have been added which give the original argument a peculiar twist.

Population expansion has not yet outstripped resources, and the famines predicted by the Malthusians failed to materialize. Nonetheless, even affluent countries cannot provide adequate shelter and 'habitat', so that a general 'housing famine' prevails.[44] A great part of the world's population is undernourished and poorly clothed, notwithstanding modern resources for producing means of sustenance. The exploitation of resources needs industry and technology: modern

---

[42] And even human groups are known with little aggressiveness:
compare Robert Knox Dentan, *The Semai, A Nonviolent People of Malaya*, New York, Holt, Rhinehart and Winston (1968).

[43] See V. Werner, 'l'Angoisse, la peur et la guerre', in *La paix par la Recherche Scientifique, Colloque de Novembere 1969*, Bruxelles, Institut de Sociologie (1970) pp. 23 - 84.

Compare note 213 *supra*. My article on Fear and Anxiety in International Relations there quoted was incorporated in my *Introduction to the Theory of International Relations* (Hebrew), Tel Aviv, Dvir (1969) as part of chapter 7: 'Mental Aggressiveness and Political Aggressiveness', pp. 70 - 81.

[44] See Charles Abrams, *Man's Struggle for Shelter in an Urbanizing World*, Cambridge, Mass., M.I.T. Press (1964).

technology can lead to the exhaustion of mineral resources and to a manifestation of the Malthusian equation in an aggravated form, when the supply of needed materials not only no longer expands proportionately with population growth but begins to recede. This day may seem far off in the future, but has — in some respects — already dawned. The same technology which made the enormous growth of production possible, has already polluted some of the resources of air, land and livestock. Huge oil tankers wreak havoc on fishes and birds, whose numbers have already been decimated by indiscriminate fishing and hunting practices and poisonous industrial waste.[45]

Living conditions in cities in developed countries have deteriorated to the point of becoming intolerable. This may hit young and old alike, but the frustrations work in particular on the emotions of the young for whom the future seems to hold nothing but grim prospects. This may — and probably does — lead as much to negative international attitudes as to local proneness to disturbances. Enough explosive tension is building up in this way as to upset the possibility of projecting continuous regional development patterns.[46]

Notwithstanding the tremendous possibilities inherent in improved agricultural 'seeds of change' which brought about a 'green revolution';[47] notwithstanding the medical inventions which may facilitate birth control — at least for those not hampered by religious or other traditional taboos; and notwithstanding improved scientific evaluation of available resources and trends, the delicate balances and the

---

[45] Compare Charles Boasson, 'Resources of the Sea and International Law', (1971) 6, *Israel Law Review*, pp. 291 - 308.
And see Richard Falk, *This Endangered World* New York, Random House (1971) who speaks of 'environmental overload'.
[46] Notwithstanding the stimulating model of Walter Isard and Stanislaw Czamanski, 'A Model for the Projection of Regional Industrial Structure, Land Use Patterns and Conversion Potentialities', (1966) Vol. V, *Papers of Peace Research Society* (Isternational) 1 - 13 and notwithstanding those authors' *caveat* that adjustments may have to be made, their appraisal seems too mechanical to include the disturbing factor of 'intolerable living conditions'.
[47] See Lester R. Brown, *Seeds of Change, The Green Revolution and Development in the 1970's*, New York, Praeger (1970).

uncertainties in the geographical, political, and population situation remain as difficult to define as ever.[48]

9. Development

The term 'development' has acquired a technical connotation in international relations literature, which is reflected in the solemn proclamations of the first and second 'development decades'.

Most of the points originally raised in this book, although written early in the first development decade, still bear repetition. As to many specific aid-for-development requirements however, much deeper insights have, naturally, been gained over the years and these are reflected in the extensive subsequent literature.

Two recent reports are particularly relevant and valuable: one by the commission on international development under the chairmanship of Lester B. Pearson and the other the study of the capacity of the U.N. development system by Sir Robert G. A. Jackson (49).

Let me first restate some of my previous suggestions:

a No one has adequately defined 'over-development'; (*supra*, Chapter III, 3c, p. 40)

b Technical development is not likely to equalize, *but rather to accentuate* the advantages prevailing in some regions or populations (*supra* Chapter III, 3 b. p. 39)

c Technical development requires social preparedness, a minimum

---

[48] See *supra* Chapter III, 3. pp. 36 - 43.
For a well considered recent exposition see: Bruce M. Russett, 'The Ecology of Future International Politics' (1967), XI *International Studies Quarterly*, 12 - 31; reprinted in: James N. Rosenau, *op. cit.* note [37] pp. 93 - 103.
Compare also: Clifton R. Wharton Jr., 'The Green Revolution, Cornucopia or Pandora's Box?' 47 (1969) *Foreign Affairs*, pp. 464 - 476.
E. Walter Coward Jr. and Wayne A. Schutjer, The Green Revolution: Initiating and Sustaining Change', XX (1970) 4 *Civilisations* (Bruxelles) pp. 473 - 484.
[49] The Pearson Report is conveniently available in a paperback edition:
Lester B. Pearson *et al. Partners in Development*, New York, Praeger (1969).
The Jackson Report, an outstanding U.N. document, deserves much wider publicity, if only as to its main conclusions, than the official U.N. publication: *A Study of the Capacity of the U.N. Development System*, Geneva, U.N. DP/5 (1969) is likely to get.

educational level; social preparedness goes hand in hand with political maturity, which means partly education and partly sheer tradition; (*supra* Chapter III, 3 b, p. 39)
d Concrete steps must be taken to change the world's present 'market' consisting of some ten or so major industrial centers, each around a more or less autonomous base. to a much more expanded and better guided market, with about thirty five major centers; (*supra* Chapter III, 3 d, p.65)
e The idea of 'aid' contains a dangerous conception — it never involves the abdication of a privileged position (*supra* Chapter III, 3 f p. 67)

The following comment on these five points seems appropriate:
(*a*): 'Over-developed' might somehow be measurable by the increasing pollution and the decreasing habitability of the larger cities (see also the previous section 8). Regions which are over-developed in this respect may show conspicuous lack of proper development in other ways, such as a housing famine or serious shortages in the educational system.

We are better informed now, at the early stage of this second development decade, about the nature of many development needs and the factors promoting development in a desired direction. In this respect the two reports just mentioned are superb. Beyond intuitive insights they contain the essence of lessons of experience. To some extent this experience was, indeed, bitter and 'must give cause for concern', but it 'should not give cause for despair'.[50] More desperate may seem the lack of insight, or, in so far any insight exists, the escapist attitudes towards the changes urgently needed on the part of and inside the more 'developed' countries. If we have, at least, been liberated from the term 'underdeveloped', we still need liberation from the idea that the 'developed' countries have reached a stage which needs no radical transformations or which can, in every respect, serve as a model for the 'developing' countries. It surely can not.

(*b*): It is not enough to speak vaguely and generally about the 'wi-

[50] Jackson Report, Vol I p. 13.
Compare also Jean-Yves Calvez, *Aspects politiques et sociaux des pays en voie de développement*. Paris, Dālloz (1971).

dening gap' between rich and poor countries. The yard-stick of G.N.P. (Gross National Product' is altogether too rough: it indicates but a few (and not always the most relevant) aspects of what Bruce M. Russett aptly calls 'trends in inequality'.[51]

Neglect in matters of public health, education or simply lack of political foresight may result in a long term deterioration, which will eventually undo the technical advantages now enjoyed in a small number of privileged areas.

Moreover technical aid by *itself* has been proven insufficient to help the aided country to overcome the bare frontiers of material inequality and *a fortiori* to be (see *Supra* Chapter III. 3, f, p.68) 'not at all a step towards world integration'. If one desires improvement in that direction, the suggestions under points (c), (d) and (e) require active heed.

(c): The need for wider educational and political synthesis are now better appreciated. Jackson quite appropriately speaks of a general 'absorptive capacity' needed for elementary economic growth.[52]

(d) and (e): The trends in technological and industrial development have been rather the reverse of what I suggested should be required.

In this respect the rich and technologically developed groups not only expand their equipment faster than others, they desire this to remain so and for this purpose they exert all their energy, attempting *not* to share with others, even to the extent of eventual social harm to themselves. In this respect one should critically analyse the European phenomenon of the so called 'guest-workers' brought in from countries starved of the necessary industries into the factories of giant industries fighting for their monopolistic position. This system may lead to troubles comparable to those resulting today from the import of

---

[51] Bruce M. Russett, *Trends in World Politics*, New York, Macmillan (1965) chapter 7, pp. 106 - 124. Russett makes, even in this summary exposition, valuable distinctions and his comparisons between groups of countries as well as health and cultural activities are quite revealing.

[52] The Jackson Report *op. cit.* Note [48] Vol. I p. 32 and Vol. II chapter V, pp. 434ff.

See also Lucian W. Pye (ed.) *op. cit.* Note [26] *supra;*

John W. Hanson and Cole S. Brembeck (eds) *Education and the Development of Nations*, New York, Holt, Rinehart and Winston (1966).

African slaves into the United States at the time. Neither industrial leaders nor their governments seem to care. A major chance to plan a better and more humanly harmonized worldwide market network has been lost and nothing achieved but the injustifiable hardships of temporary population-transplantations. The above phenomenon shows how self-satisfied attitudes go well together with international 'aid'.

It would be a good thing for International Relations theory if political scientists in the 'developed' countries would appreciate and also teach the widest possible audience how distant their own countries, their cultures and political systems, are from the higher goals to which the best of mankind aspire.

Indeed, all development — in the non-technical sense as well as in the technical sense — is affected by the planning thereof and by the goals set to at least *some* extent. To evaluate, on the basis of insight in the factors involved, the *actual* extent to which this is so, belongs to the most baffling of theoretical and practical problems. Not every lofty goal is helpful and no planning achieves its goal without adequate response. Nevertheless, the study of international relations is only scientific and worthwhile if it enables us to consider how planning towards a better world could evoke the optimum positive response.

Jerusalem

January — March 1971

INDEX OF AUTHORS REFERRED TO

Abel, T., 89
Abrams, Charles, 117
Abt, Clark C., 108
Alger, Chadwick F., 114
Alker, Hayward R., 112
Allsop, K., 43
Almond, G. A., 89
Angell, R. C., 44, 86
Ardrey, Robert E., 116
Aron, R., 25, 26, 44, 86
Ashworth, W., 70

Bacon, Francis, 101
Baker-Fox, Annette, 32
Banfield, E., 106
Barents, J., 83
Barr, S., 68
Barth, K., 21
Barzun, J., 47
Beloff, M., 50, 83
Beaufre, 107
Belshaw, H., 69
Berlin, I., 18
Bernal, J. D., 65, 66, 71
Bernard, Jessie, 44, 86, 88, 89
Berthold, F., 21
Bixenstine, V. Edwin, 104
Boasson, Ch., 5, 14, 35, 38, 40, 42, 52, 54, 64, 81, 86, 99, 103, 108, 117, 118
Bodde, D., 1
Bossard, J. H., 35
Boulding, Kenneth E., 105, 106, 107
Bouthoul, G., 42
Brecht, A., 8, 20
Brembeck, Cole S., 121
Brierly, J. L., 55

Brockway, F., 59
Brodie, B., 107
Brody, Richard A., 114
Brown, Lester R., 118
Bruck, H., 76
Buber, M., 21
Buck, P. W., 30
Burns, Arthur Lee, 113
Butler, D. W., 84
Butterfield, Herbert, 105

Calvez, Jean-Yves, 120
Cantril, H., 89
Carr, E. H., 24, 25, 26
Charlesworth, J. C., 106
Christiansen, B., 13
Claude, I. L., 90
Clausewitz, Carl von, 105
Cohen, B., 77
Cohen, M., 23
Cole, J. P., 36
Coward, E. Walter, 119
Cottrell, W. F., 5, 42
Cressey, G. B., 38
Crossmann, R. H. S., 82
Crotty, William J., 112
Czamansky, Stanislaw, 118

Dahl, R., 73
Dallin, A., 35
Davison, W. Philip, 110
De Bourbon-Busset, J., 27
De Castro, J., 69
De Madariaga, S., 64
Den Haan, J., 43
Denker, Rolf, 116
Dennett, R., 35

Dentan, Robert Knox, 117
Deutsch, K. W., 7, 27, 112, 113
De Visscher, Ch., 52
Ditman, R., 43
Dray, W., 86, 87
Duyker, H. C. J., 88

Easton, D., 72
Edel, A., 20
Edinger, L. J., 7, 113
Erickson, John, 109
Eysenck, H. J., 84

Fagen, Richard R., 111
Falk, Richard, 118
Finlay, David J., 111
Fisher, R. A., 14
Fitz Simmons, M. A., 27, 33
Fox, W. T. R., 2, 24, 29
France Anatole, 46, 49
Frankel, J. L., 85
Free Lloyd A., 110
Frisch, Otto von, 116
Fryda, N. H., 88
Fuller, C. D., 3, 36
Furniss, E. S., 77
Fyot, J. L., 67

Galbraith, J. K., 41, 62, 66
Gandhi, L., 108
Gardner, R. N., 69
Gini, C., 42
Ginsburg, N., 40
Golembiewski, Robert T., 112
Goodspeed, S. S., 3
Graham, J. J., 105
Greene, Th. M., 20
Guetzkow, Harold, 114, 115

Haesaert, J., 52
Hall, S., 66
Hanson, John W., 121
Harkabi, Y., 107
Harries, O., 31
Harris, S. E., 69

Hartley, E. L., 12
Hartshorne, R., 40
Hayter, W., 34
Heilperin, M. A., 67
Hertzler, J. O., 42
Herz, John H., 116
Hilsman, R., 28
Hobbes, 73, 82
Hoffman, Arthur S., 110
Hoffmann, S. H., 8, 77, 81
Hohenberg, John, 110
Holsti Ole R., 111
Holzner, B., 88
Howard, Michael, 105
Huber, M., 53
Huizinga, J., 45
Hull, C., 69
Huntington, E., 38

Inkeles, A., 88
Isard, Walter, 118

Jackson, H., 43
Jackson, Robert G. A., 52, 119, 120, 121
Jervis, Robert, 111
Jessup, Ph. C., 57
Johnson, J. E., 35
Jooss, K., 31
Juvenalis, 82

Kaplan, M., 81, 82
Kaufmann, W., 9, 49
Keller, A. G., 62
Kelsen, H., 14
Kertesz, S. D., 27, 33
Kessler, Allan, 114
Kindleberger, Ch. P., 70
Kirk, G., 3, 7, 75
Kissinger, Henry A., 107
Klineberg, O., 88
Knorr, Klaus, 109
Kohr, L., 71
Kranenburg, R., 73

Kristensen, Th., 71

Landheer, B., 70
Lasswell, H. D., 7, 41, 72, 76, 89, 91, 112
Lauterpacht, H., 52, 55
Lazarsfeld, L., 14
Leonard, L., 3
Leonard, Roger Ashley, 105
Lerner, D., 7, 27, 39, 71, 110, 111
Levinson, D. J., 88
Levitt, Clifford A., 104
Lewin, K., 12
Lincoln, G. A., 7
Lindzey, G., 88
Liska, G., 80
Locke, 82
Lorenz, Konrad, 116
Luard, Evan, 106
Lüschen, Günther, 104

Machiavelli, 73
MacIntyre, A., 49
MacIver, R. M., 59
Macrides, Ray C., 113
McNeil, Elton B., 115
Mangone, G. J., 44
Mannheim, K., 13, 47
Manning, C. A. W., 3
Manning, Robert, 110
Macro Polo., 36
Markham, S. F., 37
Mathisen T., 43
Maude, F. N., 105
Mayo, E., 63, 91
Meade, J. E., 67
Meyer, R. L., 40, 41
Merriam, Ch. E., 72, 74, 76
Merrit, Richard L., 112, 113
Miller, William Robert, 108, 109
Montesquieu, 73
Morgenthau, H., 4, 5, 6, 7, 30, 33
Moseley, Ph. E., 35
Murphy, G., 12
Myrdal, G., 68

Naeland, Robert C., 114
Nagel, E., 94
Naville, Denise, 105
Naville, Pierre, 105
Newcomb, Th. M., 12, 15
Nietzsche, F., 49
Nogee, Joseph L., 108
Nordfelt, H., 63
Numelin, R., 59

Ogburn, W. F., 40
Oppenheim, L., 55

Packard, V., 41
Padelford, N. J., 7
Parsons, T., 41, 78
Pear, T. H., 44, 86
Pearson, Lester B., 119
Polo, Marco, 36
Poole, D. C., 83
Popper, K. R., 48, 49
Presser, J., 18
Pruit, Dean, G., 102
Pye, Lucien W., 111, 121

Queener, L., 13

Renier, G. J., 49
Robbins, L., 62
Robbins, R., 90
Robinson, A., 67
Rokan, Stein, 11
Röling, B. V. A., 55
Röpke, W., 64, 66
Rosenau James N., 116, 119
Rosenbaum, Naomi, 114
Rothaus, Paul, 104
Russett, Bruce M., 51, 112, 119, 121
Ruyssen, Th., 50

Sapin, B., 76
Schelling, Th. C., 90, 97, 109
Schramm, Wilbur, 111
Schutjer, Wayne A., 119
Shaw, G. B., 59

Sherif, M., 12
Shubak, M., 90
Singer, J. D., 40, 108, 113
Snyder, R., 4, 76, 77, 90
Snyder, Richard C., 5, 114, 115
de Sola Pool, Ithiel, 114
Sorokin, P. A., 48
Spanier, John, W., 108
Sprott, W. J. H., 77
Sprout, H. and Margaret, 37, 38
Stenuit, Robert, 116
Stone, J., 14, 52, 53, 56, 57, 103
Summer, W. G., 62
Swinth, Robert L., 104
Swift, R. N., 36

Taber, Robert, 109
Tabouis, Genevieve, 110
Taft, D. R., 90
Talmon, J. L., 18
Taylor, G., 37, 40
Thompson, E. P., 49, 66
Thompson, K. W., 32
Tolstoy, Leo, 45, 75
Travis, M. B., 30
Truc, G., 73

Van der Molen, Gesina, 55
Vandyke, Vernon, 106
Veblen, Th., 65

Verney, D. V., 84
Visher, S. S., 37
Vitoria, F., 50, 51
Vlekke, B. H. M., 1
Von Mises, L., 63

Wallace, Donnel, 104
Wallas, G., 84
Waltz, K. N., 4
Ward, A. D., 20
Wedge, Bryant, 110
Weiller, J., 67
Weisskopf, W. A., 62
Welsh, William A., 112
Wengler, W., 30
Werner, V., 117
Wharton, Clifton R., 119
White, Howard, B., 101
Wight, Martin, 105
Williams, J. B., 67
Williams, R. M., 80
Wilson, Kellogg, V., 104
Wolf, Ch., 69
Wolfers, A., 29
Wolfle, D., 41
Woolf, L., 45
Wright, Q., 5, 42, 58, 78, 79, 97

Young, W., 1
Yu-lan, F., 1